The World's
my Oyster

Book 2

Daz Tait

Fortis
Publishing Services

First Edition 2020 Fortis Publishing Services

Cover art: Nathalie Cauvi

ISBN-13: 978-1-9163212-4-3

Fortis Publishing
Kemp House
160 City Road
London
EC1V 2NX

Dedication

This book is dedicated to Craig Tait and Craig Arnold. If it wasn't for my two brothers, then this book would never have seen the light of day.

Acknowledgements

Firstly, I must thank my family for always supporting me in whatever I endeavour to do. It means the world to me that however far I travel, I will always have a home to come back to wherever you are.

Thank you to the Sagres Crew who helped me in my time of need after I got shipwrecked in Portugal, each and every one of you deserves a medal.

To the World Atlantic Rally for Cruisers and their workers, collectively known as the yellow shirts, your efforts to organise an amazing rally around the world were incredible. A special thanks to Mark Burton for his advice whenever I needed some technical stuff reviewed in the book.

To Bobby and Harry (names changed as what I had to say about them wasn't always positive), we may not have always seen eye to eye but thank you for inviting me to sail on your yachts. Massimo and the crew aboard Giampi, I hope we get to cruise the world's oceans together again soon.

Sheila, it wouldn't have been half the adventure without you by my side so thank you for making the first half of my journey around the world so memorable.

Thank you to Stephen and Belle Feast, Matthew Dibble and Craig Arnold for looking after me in Australia as well as innumerable people I met along the way from Las Palmas to Darwin, your kindness and hospitality were what made the trip so special.

A huge thank you must go to Ken Scott, my writing coach, and Anne Kennedy, my editor, who have both taught me the skills to write, and helped me produce a story that I am very proud of. My gratitude to Nathalie Cauvi for taking the time to hand paint the beautiful, unique book covers for the whole trilogy.

Lastly, to Reinette Visser at Fortis Publishing for her continued support. I look forward to a long and successful partnership.

I never thought that writing about sailing around the world would be harder than the circumnavigation itself, but take my word for it, it was. I hope you enjoy reading my books as much as I enjoyed writing them.

Follow my adventures!

www.daztait.com

The full-colour versions of the photos in this
book, and more, are available on my website.

Table of Contents

Chapter 1

Round Two

It was precisely a year to the day I'd been shipwrecked in Portugal. I was back in the UK, visiting my mum and I'd just finished a Skype interview with a skipper intending to sail around the world. He was looking for crew to help him sail from Las Palmas in the Canary Islands all the way to Australia on the World ARC (Atlantic Rally for Cruisers) and I'd got the gig.

I ran into the kitchen, picked my Mum up and spun her around in the air.

'Woohoo! I'm going back to sea,' I squealed in delight, 'and this time I'm going to make it all the way around the world!'

The two weeks post shipwreck in Portugal was a traumatic experience. As well as having to deal with the emotional turmoil of losing my beautiful boat, there was also the uncertainty of my future. My whole world had been turned upside down and I did the only thing I could to try and forget the torment and pain - I buried myself in work.

From sunrise to sunset, I grafted like a Trojan, trying to salvage my belongings and anything else of value not yet destroyed by the ocean as everything I owned in the world got pounded twice a day by the incoming tide. It was initially a mad dash to get as much of my gear out of the wreckage as possible and stashed on higher ground. Within two days of Pablo informing me that Hitrapia was lost, the beach looked like a refugee camp, with my pitched tent and salt-encrusted possessions strewn everywhere above the tide's high waterline.

Sails, surfboards, clothes, books, tools, spares and all the electronics that hadn't been submerged in seawater; everything had to be removed. Once I saved what I could from the sea, I trudged it the two hundred metres along the beach to a warehouse the local boatyard owner had lent me for storage. There I dumped the damp contents of what was left of my life on the workshop's oily concrete floor. I then painstakingly washed each item with freshwater and hung everything out to dry. After each exhausting day I retired to my tent on the beach, thirty metres from the shipwreck, only to be woken up most nights as nefarious locals descended onto the carcass of Hitrapia and tried to plunder whatever was left behind. I chased them off, knowing they'd be back again and almost lost my self-control one morning when I woke up to see two young children clambering all over the wreck while their parents stood by laughing.

'What do you think this is?' I screamed at the adults, 'A fucking jungle gym!'

They didn't understand a word I said, but they got the message loud and clear and beat a hasty retreat. My beautiful boat turned into a kid's play park; their disrespect galled me for days.

It was a recurring nightmare that continued until I'd stripped the boat bare. Other than my unwelcome late-night visitors, I was surrounded throughout the experience by a bunch of amazing friends in Sagres, old and new, who helped me out immeasurably.

Jesus, Didier, Sylvia, Concha, Marta and Michaël, to name just a few. I will never be able to thank them enough for their varied assistance as I wouldn't have coped without their help. After two weeks John, the Dutch insurance surveyor who had made himself indispensable by sorting out the attempted salvage effort, organised a thirty-ton crusher. It rolled onto the beach, destroyed Hitrapia in a matter of hours and piled the mangled wreckage into two skips on the beach. The giant metal dustbins were then loaded onto the back of a truck and that was that. An ignoble end to what had once been a vessel of sublime beauty and infinite potential.

It was fortunate for me that it was a clear case of negligence on behalf of the port authority who'd rented me their mooring. They hadn't serviced the buoy for years and the chain had snapped, resulting in the total loss of my yacht. They were therefore liable for all the damages incurred.

My insurance company paid out within a month of the accident and I once again became cash-rich but boat-poor - straight back to square one. After the accident I was emotionally exhausted as it felt like my soul had been ripped from my body and I decided to get as far away from yachts as possible. I needed space and time to clear my head because losing Hitrapia felt like a bereavement. Yet, I still felt drawn to water. I still loved the ocean and didn't hold it at all accountable for the calamity that had befallen me. It had been human error, pure and painfully simple.

I decided to skip the European winter and headed to Australasia, spending a month in Sydney visiting my *adopted* brother Craig Arnold. He's an extraordinary character and one of the most positive people I've ever met - just the kind of person I needed to be around to help mend my broken heart. I then headed over to New Zealand, bought a small people carrier and converted it into a camper van. I lost myself in the mystic wilds of the North and South Islands of Aotearoa, 'The land of the long white cloud,' for five blissful months. From Auckland, I made my way down the coast, surfing and camping on untouched beaches all the way to the southern fjords and Milford Sound. From lush, fertile vineyards to the soaring mountains known as the Southern Alps, New Zealand has some of the most spectacular scenery I've ever seen. All of this beauty is compressed into two little islands, filled with a population that is so friendly, it's almost offensive. It is one of the most beautiful and unspoilt places I've ever had the privilege of exploring and just the salve I needed for my devastated soul.

During this time the pain of losing my yacht lessened, but at the back of my mind there was an unshakeable feeling that I still had unfinished business to attend to. No matter how hard I tried, the thought was always with me that I'd started, but not completed, the adventure I had planned and dreamed of for fifteen years. My shattered vision of sailing around the world would forever remain on that beach in Portugal unless I did something about it. I pondered these questions late at night as I lay in my camper van staring at the Southern Hemisphere's stars. What kind of person would I be if I just gave up on my dream? Would I grow old and have regrets about what might have been? Could I look at myself in the mirror, knowing that I'd failed in my quest? There were times when I'd try and convince myself to give up on the idea, thinking it was stupid, dangerous and expensive. Then I'd recall my father's little lectures when I was younger. One, in particular, sprang to mind, and his form would come to me as clear as day. I could envisage this big, towering man, the wrinkles on his forehead pinched ever closer together as he concentrated, his words floating into my mind as if he were talking to me from the afterlife. 'A promise is a promise Darroch, if you say you're going to do something, then you get it done. No matter what happens, you must always be a man of your word.' I couldn't shake those words. My father was right.

I had promised myself I was going to sail around the world, so I put any thoughts of quitting out of my mind. I ventured back to Europe when it got too cold in the Southern Hemisphere and did my normal two months Swiss summer school stint. By the end of summer I'd had enough time to lick my wounds and it was time to get back to sea. I thought long and hard about buying another yacht, but my mind kept going back to a conversation I'd had with Alan on my first transatlantic crossing. When I mentioned I was going to buy a boat and sail around the world, he'd laughed out loud.

'Don't be stupid boy, sail other people's yachts, it's much cheaper.'

The more I thought about it, the more I realised how much sense it made. I didn't have a limitless budget and knew from experience how expensive yachts could be. It was time to try a different tack. I decided to crew on other people's boats and attempt to sail around the world that way instead.

I flew into Las Palmas at the beginning of November 2015, laden down with sixty kilograms of luggage. You know you've brought too much stuff when the airline charges you more for your second bag than they did for your flight and first bag combined, but the circumnavigation would take in all the seasons, so I packed for every eventuality.

Las Palmas felt familiar as it had only been three years since I first landed there in search of a yacht to take me across the Atlantic, but I was wiser and way more experienced than back then. One thing hadn't changed though - adrenalin still coursed through my veins at the thought of setting out to sea again. Sailing under an unknown captain would be a challenging experience as I'd spent eighteen months as the skipper of my own boat, but it was a trade-off I'd just have to get used to.

Bobby, the owner and skipper of my new boat, met me on the dock next to Free Spirit. She was a Jeaunneau Sun Odyssey 54DS and his pride and joy. Bobby was a short, jovial, middle-aged character of medium build who exuded a charisma and vitality that was quite endearing. He welcomed me aboard and introduced me to the other two crew members, Joern and Michael, who'd arrived earlier in the week and were busy with various jobs. After a quick handshake, I stowed my belongings in my cabin and went straight to work. With only five days until the start of the rally, there were still a ton of jobs to complete before the yacht was ready for an ocean crossing.

We all worked extremely hard during the daylight hours, then settled down to some proper drinking in the evenings. It's imperative to get to know the people you're about to go sailing with before you set off on a voyage, and the surest route to cementing these critical relationships, in the shortest possible time, is to lubricate conversations with a lot of alcohol.

Even though Free Spirit was a fifty-four-foot yacht, it was still a small space for four people to live in for almost three weeks at sea, so we all put in a big effort to bond as a team. Joern, a big chunk of a Swiss guy, had vast amounts of sailing experience. A robust and dependable character, I was happy he was onboard as it's always comforting to know you're heading out to sea with at least one other person who can really handle themselves when the shit hits the fan. Michael, on the other hand, was a retired doctor and not particularly experienced in sailing matters, other than in the art of astronavigation. His primary reason for the voyage was to use his sextant – a navigational instrument measuring the angular distance between two objects - to calculate our position on the ocean from the sun and stars. This was great news for me. Astronavigation was a nautical skill I'd been dying to understand yet I hadn't sailed with anybody capable or willing to teach it to me. Michael seemed more than happy to pass on his knowledge of this arcane art, so I was doubly excited about the upcoming crossing. Bobby was an interesting one. Although not an experienced skipper, he was intelligent and he was knowledgeable about the theoretical side of sailing and focused on problem-solving. He also wasn't averse to spending his money on equipment required for the trip. Unless you've owned a boat, you won't understand how expensive it is to run one - and the bigger the boat, the bigger the problems and the hungrier the black hole for your hard-earned cash gets. Bobby didn't cut any corners with regard to expenses on the yacht, and after the first few days I developed a healthy respect for his organisational abilities.

Through the loss of litres of blood, sweat and tears we got the boat ready in time for the official start of the ARC+ (the Atlantic Rally for Cruisers that goes via the Cape Verde Islands) with an hour to spare.

We manoeuvred well and hit the start line of the rally in the top five out of a fleet of over sixty yachts and it became immediately apparent that Bobby was in it to win it. It was definitely a race for him and not the easy-going rally it was initially intended to be. The fundamental difference between these two approaches to sailing is that a racer's mindset is always to push the boat to its limit for extra speed. This means more sail up in stronger winds, for longer periods of time, increasing the level of risk of an accident for both the yacht and her crew.

On the other hand, a cruiser's mindset is to mitigate as much of the inherent risk in sailing as possible, by not straining the boat or placing unnecessary demands on the crew. This means a far more conservative approach where safety trumps speed every time. These two opposing approaches to a long ocean passage put Bobby and me at odds with each other from the start. I love taking risks and going to ridiculous lengths to scare myself half to death, just not when I'm sailing. When I sail, I am completely risk averse. The sea is such a treacherous environment that I see no need to make it any more dangerous than it already is, especially when crossing oceans where you can be weeks away from any kind of assistance if things go wrong.

Local fisherman plying their trade

During the first couple of days, I frequently advocated reefing the sails early and dropping the spinnaker (the vast, billowing sail that is flown from the bow of the boat) at the first sign of inclement weather, but Bobby preferred to push on until the last possible moment.

I felt this was reckless and endangered us all. Still, we arrived safely in Mindelo after six days without any catastrophes. Mindelo is the port city on São Vicente, in the volcanic archipelago of Cape Verde, situated off the west coast of Africa. It's made up of colourful colonial houses set against a backdrop of low-lying rugged mountains. A quaint little place but in need of some tender loving care as it is dirt poor and run down.

We only had a couple of days to explore this vibrant little city that's famous for its Creole Afro-Portuguese cultural mix. Cape Verde was first colonised by the Portuguese in the fifteenth century and used as a base for their slave trade. With the mingling of many different ethnic groups, it's not uncommon to see beautiful, dark-skinned women with blond hair and piercing blue eyes or light-skinned women sporting afros. I managed to buy some decent fishing lures and we visited a couple of the nearby islands. However, it was only a short stopover before we headed out to sea again.

As the voyage progressed we only encountered the occasional light squall during the day and nothing adverse at night so my conservative outlook started to fall on deaf ears. At the beginning of the trip we agreed to put one reef in the mainsail before sundown every night, but this fell by the wayside as we found ourselves sitting in third position in our race class after ten days at sea. The old sailing adage holds that *there can only be one skipper onboard*, so I had to bite my tongue and accept that my advice, at times, was blatantly ignored. It was Bobby's boat; he was the captain and the final decision was always going to be his.

It was around midnight on the tenth night and I was off watch and sound asleep in my cabin when I was woken up by a change in the rhythm of the boat. It's incredible how attuned you become to your environment after spending some time at sea and I'd immediately sensed the boat's acceleration. Seconds later I heard Joern shouting down the companionway,

'Daz, get up here quick!'

I jumped out of bed and sprinted up the companion way and into the cockpit as the boat lurched forward. The wind strength doubled from fifteen to thirty knots in a matter of seconds and the boat charged forward. 'Squall!' Joern shouted at me over the screaming wind, 'reef the foresail!'

With the wind coming from directly behind we were sailing in a goose-wing configuration. Goose winging means you have the main sail and boom out to one side of the boat and the foresail - attached to a metal pole from the mast to keep it taut - flying on the opposite side of the boat. Also called wind-to-wing, this sail configuration creates a massive sail area for downwind sailing. It's a powerful way to sail as you harness all the wind's strength, but it can be dangerous for exactly the same reason.

Fortunately we had an electric winch and I managed to reef the foresail quickly, leaving about a third of the sail out. This reduced the pressure on the mast from the powerful winds but still kept the boat balanced so Joern could steer. Ten seconds later, the full brunt of the squall hit us with a gut-wrenching scream and the boat took off down the waves. Joern clung to the wheel with all of his considerable might as I wedged myself next to him and kept my eye on the anemometer, the instrument that indicates the wind's direction and strength.

'Forty knots mate, steer to starboard twenty degrees,' I shouted over the cacophony of wind and salty sea spray.

When sailing goose-winged it's crucial to keep the wind as close to directly behind the boat as possible. If Joern steered too far to starboard (the right-hand side), he'd back the foresail (when the wind catches the wrong side of the sail), causing the boat to swing to the right, bringing the waves crashing directly onto the beam of the boat and swamping us. An even worse outcome was if Joern steered too far to port (the left-hand side) and the wind caught the back of the mainsail, causing an accidental gibe. This is when the entire weight of the boom and mainsail swings from one side of the boat to the other. Pushed on by the full fury of the wind the boom accelerates through its arc and smashes into the rigging on the opposite side of the boat with enough force to destroy the mainsail, snap the boom and even dismast the yacht, bringing the whole rig down on top of the crew. An extremely dangerous and potentially life-threatening situation, and something to be avoided at all costs.

'Forty five knots buddy, steer to port...to port, hold it there,' I bellowed as the wind continued to increase. 'Fifty knots mate, back to starboard,' I screamed as I grabbed the second helm (Free Spirit had a wheel on either side of the boat for steering) and pushed with all my might to help change direction. It was beginning to get scary as I wasn't sure how much more wind the full main sail could take. I glanced across to see Joern's granite form straining against the full force of nature, legs well spread for balance, gazing intently ahead in total concentration as he tried to maintain the course I'd set. It was an awe-inspiring sight and I was thankful the two of us were strong and competent enough to face this brutal test together. I could only spare a second though and my eyes shot straight back to the anemometer so I could continue to relay the wind switches and various course adjustments to Joern. It was back and forth as the wind and waves battered the boat, requiring one hundred percent concentration from the two of us to keep Free Spirit sailing within the very tight wind angles we had to maintain. Any deviation from our course would have been catastrophic and we both knew that the boat and our lives were at stake. It felt like an eternity before the wind gradually receded and life aboard returned to a semblance of normality. The worst of the squall had only lasted for fifteen minutes but in that short time, Joern and I had become fast friends. The foundation of any strong sailing relationship is built on mutual respect gained through witnessing a person's competence and reliability. We'd survived the storm together through quick actions and teamwork and that's what the fellowship of sailing is all about.

We both sat down after the gruelling trial and congratulated each other on a job well done. 'That was brutal Joern, you helmed like a pro,' I said. 'I couldn't have done it without you Daz,' he replied in a solemn voice, 'your steering corrections were essential. That's one of the worst squalls I've ever experienced.'

'Yeah, the top gust was fifty-seven knots,' I replied, 'it was nuts. I've never experienced that much of the wind's power before.'

He nodded slowly.

'The boat handled it pretty well,' he said, 'but I'm glad you were quick enough to furl the foresail or it may have been a different story.'

'Where the hell was Bobby,' I asked, 'why wasn't the skipper up on deck in a flash?'

Bobby's cabin was in the bow of the boat and it was improbable he'd slept through that rollercoaster ride, but if he had, then that was even more worrying. It indicated he had absolutely no idea of the magnitude of danger we'd just faced and any skipper worth his salt would have checked to see everything was under control.

'Bobby is a boat owner, not a skipper.' Joern replied. 'As I'm sure you already know, there's a huge difference between the two.'

I stayed with Joern in the cockpit for the next two hours until the end of his watch when Michael came up to relieve us. We explained to Michael what had happened and told him not to release any more of the double reefed foresail during his watch, just in case another squall hit us during the night. With the boat well-trimmed and sailing along comfortably, a tired Joern and me hit the sack in need of some well-deserved rest.

A couple of hours later my sleep was once again disrupted but this time in a far more violent manner. I woke up flying through the air, coming to an abrupt halt as I slammed into my cabin door and slid down onto the floor. Bleary eyed and confused about what could possibly have happened - my initial thought was that we had hit a whale or a submerged container - I stumbled into the cockpit to witness all hell had broken loose. Michael was sitting by the helm in total shock with the whites of his eyes showing, clearly overwhelmed by the situation. I looked up in horror to see that the boom was on the starboard side. We had accidentally gibed. The immense force created as the sail swung through one hundred and eighty degrees had snapped the preventer line and ripped the main sheet's fittings out of the deck. The entire foresail was flogging away on the starboard side too, still attached to the booming out pole.

'What the fuck,' I shouted, 'who ...…'

I didn't have time to finish the sentence because the six-metre aluminium booming out pole, weighing around twenty kilograms, had snapped in half from the wind pressure and was wickedly swinging around the foredeck in search of something to impale. It was all hands-on deck and took an hour of frantic actively to secure the boat from sustaining any more damage.

It took the rest of the day for the whole story of what transpired that morning to come out. Bobby had wandered up on deck during Michael's watch and was unhappy that Joern and I had slowed the boat down. It was unclear how much information Michael had relayed to him about the initial squall Joern and I had fought, but either way, Bobby decided to unfurl the full foresail in the goose-wing configuration once again. About an hour later another ferocious squall hit, but this time they hadn't been quick enough to furl the foresail. With all the canvas out, the wind propelled the boat headlong into the sea, the helmsman lost control, Free Spirit slewed to port and the boom flew across the boat as we accidentally gibed. This episode just highlighted the danger of taking a racing mentality to sea when you cannot back it up with experience and skill. When things go wrong on a boat, they do so quickly and in a big way. Bobby paid the price for getting too cocky and we limped into St Lucia a week later, languishing in the middle of the fleet, with a yacht in need of numerous repairs.

Chapter 2

A Caribbean Christmas

Although we experienced our fair share of mayhem on the Atlantic crossing, it was still incredible to circle once again around the top of Pigeon Island, on the north western tip of St Lucia, and head into Rodney Bay. Three years had passed since I'd first landed on those iridescent shores, but it felt as if I'd never left as I recognized the familiar landmarks etched in my memory.

After two weeks at sea, surrounded by nothing but blue in every direction, the first glimpse of a swaying palm tree sent a thrill of excitement through me as the enormity of what I'd accomplished sunk in. Nothing beats the feeling of knowing you've used the power of nature's wind to cross an ocean, escape a cold European winter and drop anchor in a sun-drenched Caribbean island.

Our days were filled with friends, fun and rum and nobody was in a hurry to get anything done. Affectionately referred to as 'Caribbean Time,' the pace of life slowed down to a crawl and you just kick back, relax and chill.

As our affable fisherman informed us on arrival, 'this is St Lucia maaan… not Russia, we're in no rush 'ere!'

We didn't hang around St Lucia for too long though as Bobby planned to pick up some friends in Guadeloupe in time for Christmas Day. As soon as the snapped pole was repaired and replacement parts fitted (at considerable expense to Bobby), we wished both Joern and Michael a fond farewell. They'd only signed on to cross the Atlantic and with only Bobby and me aboard, we started island hopping north up the island chain of the Lesser Antilles. On my previous Caribbean voyage I explored all the islands to the south of St Lucia. I then hitched a lift straight to Antigua, missing out on all the isles in between, so it was great opportunity to join up the rest of the dots.

Our first stop was Martinique - which in conjunction with Guadeloupe – is a French overseas department and part of the French Republic in every way imaginable. From using the Euro, to Parisian coffee shops and bakeries with baguettes filled with Brie and Camembert, it felt rather strange to be surrounded by European culture right in the heart of the West Indies. We anchored in the picturesque harbour near the infamous town of Saint Pierre and once ashore, learnt the sad history of this once prominent city, formerly known around the world as the 'Paris of the West Indies.'

On the morning of the 8th of May 1902, Mount Pelée, the highest mountain on the island, volcanically erupted with incredible force, blowing off the top of the mountain and creating a huge pyroclastic cloud. This devastating cloud of a thousand-degrees Celsius super-heated gas swept down the mountain at speeds in excess of 650km an hour, destroying everything in its path, including the island's capital city of Saint-Pierre. In a matter of minutes thirty thousand people were dead, the entire city was levelled and an estimated two hundred vessels, including eighteen large ships, were sunk in the harbour. Only a handful of people survived this cataclysmic event, the most famous of whom was Auguste Cyparis, a common labourer in the town who was regularly in trouble with the authorities.

Arrested the night before the eruption and thrown into jail for murdering a man during a street fight, he was placed in solitary confinement and locked in a bomb proof munitions magazine built underground and, luckily for Auguste, the most secure building on the island. Although Cyparis was horribly burnt, the ventilation shaft for his cell faced away from the eruption and he miraculously survived. He was found four days later by a rescue party when he cried out in anguish. He subsequently recovered, was pardoned for his crime and joined the circus. Famed as 'the man who lived through Doomsday,' he toured America and become a minor celebrity years later.

But Mount Pelée wasn't quite finished yet. Less than two weeks later it erupted again, with equal ferocity, and killed the two thousand disaster relief personal sent to help rebuild the city in the wake of the initial disaster. Saint-Pierre never attained its former glory as

Fort-de-France became the capital city further south down the coast. Numerous shipwrecks still litter the bay to this day, a stark reminder of the unstoppable power Mother Nature can unleash when she's in a bad mood.

As I walked through the ruins of the 'Théatre du Petit Paris' and past Cyparis's cell, I looked up at the summit of Mount Pelée and shivered. It was a sobering thought to think that a century ago the mountain standing before me had effortlessly swept aside civilisation in an instant. To vanquish these melancholy thoughts, we headed to the oldest rum distillery on the island and sampled as much of their liquid delights as they'd allow. After our tour of the plantation, Bobby and I merrily made our way back to the boat with half a dozen bottles of rum in tow. Before I went to bed that evening, I poured a tot of rum into the sea as a salute to all those poor sailors whose lives had been so abruptly extinguished on that cataclysmic day.

Nestled between the two developed French islands is the relatively unknown island of Dominica, the poorest country in the Caribbean and our next stop. As the island is mostly volcanic, with very few beaches, it is relatively underdeveloped for tourism compared to most other Eastern Caribbean islands. There are no high-rise buildings and the locals' houses are practically in the ocean as they're built right up to the water line. With no mass tourism, the island retained an authentic aura and I fell in love with its rugged, unkempt appearance. As we motored into the harbour the laid-back vibe was epitomised by our gracious welcome from the most stoned Rastafarian I have ever met.

'Ya maan, welcome to my island,' he boomed in a huge voice which didn't match his tiny frame – one of the skinniest little men I'd ever seen, with dreadlocks down to his ankles that must have weighted as much as he did. He waved at us with one hand, blazing on a spliff the size of a cigar with the other and steering his boat with his bare foot.

'I am Mr Magic, whatever you need I can get for ya maan,' he said as he winked at me with blood shot eyes.

'Hello Mr Magic,' I called back, 'we need a mooring buoy please.'

'Follow me maan, I've got da perfect spot reserved especially for ya.'

As we meandered our way through the other yachts in the bay, I began to feel pretty woozy from the billowing cloud of smoke that enveloped the yacht as we follow our host. As I gazed forward, Mr Magic began to resemble a thin little smokestack, and I began to giggle. By the time we'd moored up tears were rolling down our cheeks as we laughed at each other laughing.

In-between cackles Mr Magic managed to splutter, 'You've got da second-hand stone brother,' as we both burst out laughing again, 'and ya most welcome maan. Do ya want to smoke with me?'

I shook my head.

'No thank you my friend, I don't smoke, but thanks for the offer. Anyway, I think I've had enough already,' I said as I wiped away my tears of laughter.

'What is there to do on this island for tourists, Mr Magic?' I asked.

'Well, if ya want to sit still then ya can smoke and drink, but if ya in da mood to move then ya can dance.'

'I was thinking more along the lines of adventures to be had. I've heard there is some good hiking here.'

He looked at me as if I had lost my mind, shrugging his shoulders while he took another long draw on his spliff. 'Ya maan, there is da second biggest boiling lake in da whole world on this island. Ya got to hike way up into da mountains, descend through da Valley of Desolation and then climb a little more to find it. Ya want me to call da Sea Cat? He organises all da tourism around here because ya need a guide to get there.'

'Sure, that sounds cool man. Let's do it.'

The next morning Mr Magic picked us up. Not surprisingly, he was puffing away on another large joint and he took us ashore to meet Sea Cat. Resplendent with his own set of impressive dreadlocks, Sea Cat warmly welcomed us into his home and offered us a drink.

'Sit, sit, my friends, help ya selves to them biscuits. Ya going need a lot of energy today as it's a seven-hour hike there and back in da blistering heat.'

While I sat munching away on the proffered snacks, Sea Cat continued.

'My assistant Alfred will be taking ya today. I've been training him for a few years now so he knows what he's doing. Ya be in good hands,' he exclaimed as he led us out to his minibus and we took off to pick up Alfred.

Alfred was a tall, lean and rather solemn looking fellow, patiently waiting for us on the side of the road. He was dressed in nothing but shorts and a vest, barefoot and bare headed with a machete in one hand

and an egg box in the other. Bobby and I, wearing hiking boots, backpacks and big sun hats, weren't quite sure what to make of him but we were committed so it was time to sweat, and sweat we certainly did. The first section of the hike was through dense primary rain forest and it was like walking through a sauna, but worse because you couldn't pop outside to cool down. With no air movement, the humidity was unbearable and I was guzzling water to stay hydrated, but Alfred didn't have a bead of sweat on his brow and refused any offer of refreshment, even though he wasn't carrying any water himself. After half an hour I was wondering how long it would take Alfred to dig my grave with his machete when he stepped into a small clearing off the path and called a halt. In front of us was a magnificent fan palm tree. All of its branches fanned out from a central nucleus, resembling the tail feathers of a peacock's train, creating a beautiful green arc ending in big herbaceous leaves that looked distinctly like those found on a banana tree.

'This da Traveller Tree,' Alfred informed us as he knelt down and bored a hole with the razor-sharp point of his blade into the base of one of the branches.

'Each one of these branches collects up to a litre of water so there is always plenty to drink in da forest if ya know where to look,' he said.

He pushed the blade in a little further and water began to cascade from the bottom of the palm tree, 'try a bit maan.'

I knelt down and took a mouthful, pleasantly surprised by how cool and sweet the water tasted.

'There are also some drinking vines but ya got to know which ones are for water and which ones are for swinging on,' he shouted in glee as he took a running jump onto a hanging vine and swung in a perfect arc up towards the sky.

For the next ten minutes Bobby and I pretended to be Tarzan, attempting to swing higher and higher into the sky without pin balling off any of the tree trunks in the way while Alfred laughed in the background. From being very taciturn at the start, once he realised that we weren't just boring, rich yachties and we just wanted to have some fun, Alfred totally opened up to us and we couldn't shut him up.

For the next two hours while we ascended the mountain, we got his whole life story. After falling in with a bad crowd in Dominica, his aunt had flown him over to England for a fresh start, but unfortunately the lure of easy money had sucked him back into a life of crime. After a couple of years of living the high life in Europe he was caught dealing cocaine and immediately deported back to Dominica. His parents disowned him and nobody was willing to give him a job due to his criminal record. With a young family to support and no prospects other than continuing to deal drugs, he was in dire straits. That was when Sea Cat - who had known him since he was a young boy - found him. He understood Alfred had made some poor life choices but decided to give him an opportunity to go straight and earn his money honestly. Alfred had never looked back and he had been working for Sea Cat's tourism business ever since, sometimes hiking up the mountain twice a day in the peak season. It was no wonder that he barely sweated and his bare feet, as tough as leather, effortlessly navigated their way through the razor-sharp volcanic rock as he chatted away incessantly.

We marched on with Alfred leading the way to the summit. Behind us was the lush, green jungle we had just hiked through, but in front was something entirely different, the aptly named 'Valley of Desolation.' From the cliffs above we made the steep and dangerous descent into the land of the lost where nothing but a few hardy shrubs survived. The valley was even hotter than the forest, stinking of rotten eggs as noxious sulphurous fumes billowed out of fissures in the jagged rocks. All around us the world bubbled and hissed as the magma, not far beneath our feet, created super-heated steam, boiling anything it touched. We explored the spluttering vents and bubbling mud pits until Alfred beckoned us over to where he was squatting on the ground. He held a little stick attached to a plastic bag filled with the eggs he'd carried up, all floating in the steaming water.

'Lunch is served,' he exclaimed as he peeled off a blackened eggshell and popped a freshly boiled egg into his mouth. We ate a couple of eggs each and they were delicious.

It was another hour, hiking past innumerable sulphur springs, scalding pools and steaming waterfalls until we crested the ridge of the final ascent and came upon a natural wonder the likes of which I'd never seen before.

Completely shrouded in a moist cloud of mist, all I could hear was the unmistakeable sound of agitated water, until a gust of wind brushed aside the steam and revealed a breath-taking sight. Encircled by steep, ragged rock was a circular pool of ominous looking greyish-blue water that was violently bubbling away at its centre. At roughly sixty metres in diameter, the lake and surrounding cliffs created a basin that resembled a giant witch's cauldron. With no safety barriers for protection from the precipitous drop-off and inhaling fumes that certainly weren't helping my balance, it felt like a precarious position to be in. I retreated from the edge as a vision of my crispy cooked corpse bobbing away in the broth below urged me to step back. From a safer vantage point I observed the magical interplay between steam, wind and the continuously boiling water as they danced together before me. Watching in wonder, I contemplated the immense forces required to keep a lake of that size perpetually boiling. We still had a brutal three-and-a-half-hour hike ahead of us to retrace our steps back to the entrance of the National Park, so we didn't hang around for too long, but it was worth every bead of sweat to get there and marvel at such a unique and mystical natural phenomenon.

The next morning Mr Magic, once again anaesthetised against the woes of the world in his own personal cloud of ganja, waved us off as we headed out of the bay and north towards the butterfly shaped island of Guadeloupe. Bobby was expecting some guests onboard for Christmas, so I jumped off the boat at Pointe-a-Pitre and headed to the little villa I'd rented for the duration of my stay, a couple of kilometres down the coast. With a balcony that overlooked a palm covered white sandy beach and the ocean only a stone's throw away, it was the perfect spot for me to unwind and enjoy some peace and quiet on my own.

Once the landlady found out I was spending Noël alone, she kindly insisted that I join her and a dozen of her friends for a Christmas Eve pool party at a house nearby. This traditional late-night feast, called Le Réveillon, consisted of lavish delicacies like foie gras and oysters, washed down with magnums of champagne. Then, out came a dozen bottles of different varieties of local rum and the party really got started. By the time I left in the small hours of Christmas morning, everyone, and that included the dog, had been in the swimming pool whether they liked it or not. Me and two other rugby playing French lads at the party made sure of that. I'm not sure what it is about rum and swimming pools, but that combination always seems to bring out the devil in me.

Bobby and I sailed back to St Lucia and had an equally memorable New Year's Eve party. Anchored in the shadow of the Piton mountains (two very distinct conical volcanic spires which are depicted on the St Lucian flag), we caught up with Nick and Laurie, the owners of a beautiful catamaran called Sea Bear. Nick and I had immediately hit it off when we had first met a couple of months before in Las Palmas through our joint love of fishing and we'd spent most of our time drinking together at every port in between. He was a happy, party loving Swede and his wife, the more 'sensible' one, was a Canadian doctor. They had sold up and set off on their dream to sail around the world. At the stroke of midnight, after numerous bottles of champagne, cigars and more rum just in case we hadn't already drunk enough, Laurie grabbed a bag of out of date flares and with a great whoosh, fired a red parachute flare towards the heavens. Red flares are distress beacons and only to be used in case of an emergency when immediate assistance is required, so it's highly illegal to set them off just for fun.

Nick, with a look of absolute bewilderment on his face, turned to her in astonishment and asked, 'What the hell are you doing?'

But at that point it was too late for any sensible thinking because we all had our hands on a flare and proceeded to light the sky up like a Christmas tree. The other boats in our vicinity all answered with flares of their own so Nick, nonplussed now, passed me the last of the handheld phosphorous flares and we set them off together to finish the year in a blaze of glory.

Letting off flares on New Year's Eve with Swedish Nick

Chapter 3

Setting off to circumnavigate

14°04'30N, 60°57'00W

With the departure of Michael and Joern there were two empty spaces on the boat and Tommy filled them with Stevie and Stevo, two chaps in their late forties. Stevie was a gentle Buddhist who meditated and I liked him from the start. He wasn't the most experienced sailor but he wanted to learn and his cooking skills were outstanding so he was a welcome addition to the crew. Stevo, on the other hand, was a yacht master instructor, a fact of which he would remind you at every available opportunity. It didn't take a rocket scientist to figure out he was going to get on my tits, but when you sail on other people's yachts, sometimes you've just got to grin and bear it.

The official start of the World Arc was at the end of the first week in January and the run up to it was filled with events and parties. I thought I'd already met most of the skippers and crews of the other thirty boats taking part in this round the world rally, so I was a little taken aback when a really striking, leggy blonde wandered onto the scene. She wore clinging jeans, a bright yellow tank top with *South Africa* emblazoned across her chest and she had one of the most intense gazes I'd ever seen. Slightly intimidating, yet alluring and intriguing all at the same time, I must admit that I was captivated from the start. After a little Dutch courage, I approached her and we began to chat. Her name was Sheila, she was from East Germany and she'd already sailed halfway around the world. Sheila had started her circumnavigation in Indonesia and made it as far as St Lucia before returning to work to earn more travel tokens. She was back to complete the last half of her voyage and I was impressed. Women who want to sail around the world are few and far between and the ones who go for it on their own and don't sail on family or friends' yachts, are rarer still. It takes a brave and dynamic woman to take on the male dominated world of ocean sailing and Sheila was both courageous and spirited. We chatted away and it quickly became clear that we shared many of the same passions, like scuba diving, kite surfing, free-diving and sailing and we both loved anything to do with the ocean. Over the next week we gravitated towards each other and a romance began to bloom.

But it wasn't all fraternising with the fairer sex as we still had a boat to prepare for our imminent crossing of the Caribbean Sea. The work flew by though as I was bursting to get going. This truly felt like the beginning of my circumnavigation and the fulfilment of the dream I'd been trying to grasp for so long. The Atlantic and Caribbean I'd seen before, but I was now about to venture towards parts unknown. After decades of pouring over maps of the world, the once distant seas, oceans, countries and continents I'd only ever imagined, all lay before me just waiting to be explored. It was all finally within my grasp and I couldn't wait to set sail on my voyage of discovery.

At 9am on the 8th of January 2016, we set off to the usual fanfare of air horns as our friends on the dock bid us farewell, but this time it felt different. I wasn't just popping over the pond for a jolly in the Caribbean before I headed back to the safety of Europe again. This was the real deal. All things being well, in a year and a half's time I'd be standing back on the very docks my mates were waving me off from, having traced an unbroken line all the way around the world. It was game on.

Bobby and I already knew Free Spirit inside and out and it didn't take the others too long to learn the ropes. Other than being pummelled by heavy winds, it was a pretty uneventful passage and we made our first landfall after five days of sailing in Santa Marta, the oldest inhabited city founded by the Spaniards in Colombia.

The city had a beautiful backdrop of Nevada de Santa Marta, an isolated mountain range separated from the famous Andes chain that runs through Columbia just 42 kilometres from the Caribbean coast. There were beaches everywhere and a relaxed, tranquil vibe that I must admit pleasantly surprised me as I had a preconception about Colombia. In my mind it was synonymous with infamous narco traffickers like Pablo Escobar and I imagined streets awash with blood from raging gang wars. Instead,

41

with the heaviest police presence I'd ever seen in any metropolis in the world, Santa Marta was by far the safest and friendliest South American city I had the pleasure of visiting on my travels.

One of the great things about participating in an organised rally like the WARC is that most of the bureaucracy and administration required for admission to each new country is all taken care of before you arrive. Instead of having to run around like a headless chicken from one government building to the next on a quest for the correct stamp or signature (which can take days when you can't speak the local language), you simply swan in, have your passport stamped and get straight onto the most important part of sailing around the world - having fun!

The other great thing about the WARC is that they organise endless parties. Arrival parties, prize giving parties, leaving parties and sometime even parties because 'we haven't had a party in a few days' kind of parties. Added to this, the owner of the marina, Mani, always wearing a pristine white suit and covered in enough gold to set up his own pawn shop, liked to party too. Mani owned all the real estate as far as the eye could see and his own private helicopter, parked on the quay, with a pilot on call 24/7. This, he informed me, was just in case he needed to check on his banana plantations in a hurry. He also owned the local restaurant and nightclub which meant I couldn't pay for a drink if I tried. I'd met him on the first night and he had taken a shine to me. I never got to know how Mani made his money, nor did I ask, but he was unbelievably generous and treated me like royalty so a debaucherous time was had by all.

The best party of the lot was the barbecue Mani organised on Bahia Concha in the Tayrona National Park. Over a hundred people, all taking part in the rally, were transported by private coach about forty kilometres out of the city. It was set on an idyllic white sandy beach fringed by rocky atolls, mangroves and pristine forests - an all-day event with no expense spared. The only thing more impressive than the gargantuan amount of food served was the amount of alcohol on offer. Throughout the day we drank ice cold beers and sipped our rums while playing cricket and beach volleyball in the baking hot sun. Whenever I was dripping with sweat, I simply dove into the glimmering sea to cool off. While the DJ played some chilled out euphoric tunes and the sun set on the most perfect of days, I truly felt blessed to be alive. I was following my dream, surrounded by friendly locals and an incredible group of fun-loving fellow sailors.

After a week it was almost time to set off again but not before the weather, backed up by some Colombian bureaucracy, gave us a little reminder who was actually in charge. An hour before the official start of the next leg of the WARC, the admiral of the Colombian Navy closed the port of Santa Marta to all non-commercial traffic due to big seas and high winds. For the average day sailor I guess it was dangerous but with the expertise on board the boats in this race, it would have been possible, although rather uncomfortable, to sail in those conditions. This was proven by Barbara Jean, one of the smallest boats in our fleet, whose skipper, Bob, had decided to set off a few hours before the official start time. But naval officers are not good at having their orders ignored by civilians, even if those civilians hadn't received the memo in the first place and a naval gunship was dispatched to herd the errant yacht back to port, much to the annoyance of Bob and his wife, Lori. They quickly found out, just as I had with the Helenic warships in Greece, that having a sense of humour isn't the most desirable character trait required when applying for a job in the navy.

The weather calmed down the next morning, as had the admiral's temperament, so he gave his blessing for the race to continue and we made our way towards the remote archipelago of the San Blas Islands off the Panamanian coast, a couple of days sailing away.

With its stunning turquoise waters, unspoiled white beaches and enough islands to visit a different one for each day of the year, I could have happily spent months exploring the myriad of tiny little isles.

We'd found another genuine paradise and I spent my days free diving with Sheila and exploring the shallows surrounding each island. It was incredible once again to have a wing-woman who loved adventure. We spent every free moment together surrounded by an abundance of tropical marine life, but skippers beware, there are many dangers lurking beneath those seemingly tranquil waters. Littered everywhere are ragged reefs and giant coral heads that will bite a chunk out of your hull if you aren't careful. This was clearly evidenced by the crumbling hulks of a few hapless yachts, permanently moored on the tops of coral banks. During our stay there was another boat that nearly joined them and we helped to drag it off an unchartered reef with our tender.

After a couple of hours of blissful swimming through coral gardens, Sheila and I would wade ashore with skin as wrinkled as a pair of raisins and sun ourselves to warm up. The indigenous Kuna Indians on the islands surrounding our anchorage are industrious folk and had set up little bars and basic restaurants. Coco-Locos were just about the only thing on offer, but I wasn't complaining as I could have drunk them all day. They consisted of freshly opened green drinking coconuts topped up to brim with rum. Alcoholic, yet rehydrating all at the same time and dangerously delicious. I think I halved the island's coconut and rum reserves, but I was happy to prop up the local economy. I could have stayed there forever but time was limited. We had planned a rendezvous in Shelter Bay in Colón, Panama, so I bid my Indian friends goodbye and we set sail again.

It's not often that the name of a place truly reflects its characteristics but in this case it most certainly did. Colón is undoubtedly the ass end of the world. With high unemployment and spiralling crime rates, gangs control the streets and it is an absolute shithole. Just forty kilometres away is Panama City, the capital, with gleaming new skyscrapers, malls and restaurants alive with shoppers and diners; a city that fancies itself as the Dubai of the Pacific. Colón seemed a million miles away with its rotting buildings on the point of collapse and raw sewage running through the streets. Recently, Hollywood filmmakers made Colón a stand-in for Haiti, the poorest country in the hemisphere. Situated on the outskirts of this shitty city is an old army base, Fort Sherman. Abandoned by the Americans twenty years ago and appropriated by the Panamanian Navy, a small proportion of the old base has been turned into a training camp for new recruits.

The rest has been left to the ravages of time. Patrolled by the armed forces and surrounded by a big barbed wire electrified fence, it's nigh on impossible to access it without permission. Sheltered by name, sheltered by nature.

Within a five-minute walk from Shelter Bay I had access to a unique and beautiful tropical rain forest. With limited human encroachment for decades, Mother Nature has reabsorbed what was once a concrete jungle of barracks and administrative buildings and practically wiped out all traces of mankind. The occasional brick wall and semblance of a tarmac road still remains, but they are covered in vines, creepers and armies of leaf cutting ants that camouflage the old wounds that humanity seems hell bent on inflicting on the natural world. It made my heart soar to see that with time and no interference from our meddling, destructive selves, the world can recover and revert to Her natural beauty. Mother Nature was here long before humans and She will be here way after we're all gone. Mankind's just a little destructive blip on Her radar and will be swept aside over the passage of time, just like all the other countless life forms that have come before us. Then life will once again appear in another infinitely beautiful form and the cycle will continue until our expanding sun wipes out the earth for good.

As I explored the forest on my own, surrounded by glittering butterflies and chirping parakeets, contemplating mankind's futility, I was fortunate enough to witness a very special event. Making its way slowly down from the rainforest's canopy towering above me, came one of the most unique animals on the planet. With a head framed by course hair resembling one of the Beetles' haircuts from the sixties, a white forehead and a black stripe of fur from eye socket to cheek, there was something distinctly mischievous about its face. Complete with a dark brown shaggy coat, tinged with greenish highlights from the algae that grew in its fur, was a brown throated three toed sloth. It was the size of a small dog, had a short tail and its four limbs each ended with three hooked claws. Pausing about ten metres above the forest floor, she slowly swivelled her head almost one hundred and eighty degrees and regarded me with glistening dark eyes. I knew she was a female because, burrowed into her straw-like fur and clutching onto her undercarriage, was the cutest little cub imaginable. With infinitely slow movements the baby sloth moved its head out from behind its mother's torso and peered at me inquisitively. I remained stock-still. After locking eyes for what felt like an eternity I gently whispered, 'Don't worry my little friends, I don't mean you any harm.'

Satisfied that I wasn't a threat, she resumed her languid progress towards the forest floor. Sloths head down to terra firm only once a week to urinate and defecate so it was a lucky encounter, even if the only reason I got to see her was because she needed to take a dump. Once the call of nature had been taken care of, they made their leisurely way back into the canopy. Climbing at a blistering three metres per minute, every movement was precise and in perfect flow, even if it was painstakingly slow. It wasn't long before they both disappeared from sight, once again perfectly camouflaged in the forest's foliage. A sedate encounter with the world's slowest moving mammal that I'll fondly remember for the rest of my life.

A couple of days later we had the privilege of visiting a tribal village belonging to the Embera Indians, the indigenous people of Panama. With their territory situated on the banks of the Chagres river and only accessible by meandering waterways, we jumped aboard a traditional dugout canoe carved from a single fifteen-metre-long tree trunk. For over an hour we made our way upriver as our pilot navigated his way through a multitude of brown watered tributaries, repeatedly scraping the bottom of the boat as he steered his cumbersome vessel through some sinuous sections a foot deep. Flanked by lush tropical trees and accompanied along the way by cormorants, cranes and kingfishers, it was a stunning journey into the heart of an untouched primary rain forest.

The Embera Indians populate the Darien region of Panama and the Choco region of Colombia but they were there way before any Spaniard ever set foot on the 'New World' and dismembered the Americas into countries.

When we arrived on the banks of their settlement, we were greeted by the sound of traditional music being played on handmade drums and pan pipes. The whole village of over a hundred inhabitants came out to welcome us as we stepped ashore. The women were dressed in brightly coloured skirts and the men wore equally bright sashes. The whole tribe was bare chested and had their torsos, arms and thighs painted in geometric shapes with a black dye. Not much taller than five foot but with stocky builds, they walked with the grace and fluidity of those taught from birth how to move in silence through the wilderness. The village consisted of thatched huts on stilts, two metres above the ground. They are elevated to protect the occupants from roving wild animals at night as well as from the torrential flooding that occurs during the wet season. There was a flattened central 'square' right in the middle of the settlement and a giant communal lodge to one side. On either end of the sandy square there was a set of football goals fashioned from bamboo poles with woven vines for nets. South Americans are crazy about soccer so I shouldn't have been surprised that the world's most popular game had even made its way into the jungle.

After an official welcome we were all invited to head inside the giant lodge with a score of chattering children in tow. Perched on rows of benches we sat and watched an exhibition of traditional dance, accompanied by loud drumming and high-pitched flute playing from a dozen male musicians while the tribe's women chanted in unison as they swirled together in intricate formations. It was a cacophony of sound and movement and I was dripping with sweat just watching them. It wasn't just the hundred percent humidity that was making me feel uncomfortable though. I felt like an alien intruding on those people's peaceful lives; a proud and productive folk reduced to performing like puppets for my entertainment. In no way do I mean to belittle their vigorous efforts in welcoming us to their home, but it shamed me to think that it was now necessary for them to prostitute themselves in this way to survive. With the encroachment of 'civilisation' and the consequent deforestation that followed, they could no longer live the self-sufficient existence they'd enjoyed for centuries. I had a lot of conflicting thoughts milling around in my mind, so I approached the head man and asked him a couple of questions. He explained that his village only hosted tourists three to four times a year during the dry season and all the money raised went to educating their children. He was rather philosophical about the whole thing and stated that the world was changing and his people had to change with it or they'd be left behind. It still saddened me reflect on how their existence had been transformed, but I surmised that if the head man had come to terms with it then so should I. With a big smile and a slap on the back, he directed me towards the feast of fried fish, plantains and fruit awaiting us for lunch, where I mulled over his words.

A young Embera Indian in a traditional dugout canoe

Chapter 4

Transiting the Panama Canal

09°16'15N, 79°55'00W

Our main reason for mooring in Shelter Bay was to deal with the bureaucracy and administration required to obtain permission for our non-commercial vessel to make its way through the Panama Canal.

The Panama Canal connects the Atlantic Ocean to the Pacific Ocean via a set of locks, saving vessels the long and dangerous voyage via Cape Horn to the south. When winds blowing from the Pacific Ocean come into contact with South America, the Andes Mountains channel the air towards the southern tip of South America, producing monstrous waves and turbulent weather almost impossible to predict, making Cape Horn one of the riskiest places in the world to sail. That makes the canal, cut through the Isthmus of Panama, one of the busiest shipping thoroughfares in the world. With a permanent backlog of ships waiting their turn to make the transit, any type of delay costs the canal owners millions of dollars an hour. It is no wonder the authorities in charge are extremely fastidious about the rules and regulations pertaining to each and every vessel attempting the journey.

Over the course of a week our yacht was measured, the engine checked, and strict instructions were issued on what was required of the skipper and crew while making the transit. To get a better feel for what we were in for, a day trip to the Gatun Locks Visitors' Centre was organised. Sheila and I jumped on a bus and after passing through numerous military checkpoints we left the safety of our compound. The road to town was spectacular, hugging the coast and offering panoramic sea views or winding its way through untouched rainforest teeming with parrots and toucans. It felt rather strange after my peaceful days of wandering through the jungle to re-join civilisation in Colon, confronted with the hustle and bustle of crazy traffic, drivers honking their horns in a mad panic to get somewhere but not moving an inch. That wasn't half as strange as the sight greeting us when we made our way onto the main road running parallel to the locks where a two-hundred-metre container ship gradually edged its way forward towards the first of the Gatun Locks. The colossal beast reared over fifteen metres out of the water with a stack of containers piled six high on its deck. Throughout my entire sailing career I had done everything in my power to stay as far away from those monsters as possible and now I was almost within touching distance of one. It was a surreal experience to have one so close and towering over me. An involuntary shudder ran down my spine as I imagined what it would feel like to have one of those titans bearing down on me at sea. They are truly colossal and an awe-inspiring sight, but each and every one of them haunts the nightmares of any cruising yachtsman.

A cargo ship navigating the first Gatun Lock

Completed in 1914, the Panama Canal is considered to be one of the seven wonders of the modern world. The sheer audacity of the project and the scale of the engineering required to pull it off is mind blowing. From the balcony of the Visitors Centre I looked down onto the two pairs of three Gatun locks, massive concrete structures stretching for over two kilometres. Each lock can accommodate a vessel just shy of three hundred metres long (the length of three football fields) and thirty-two metres wide. The locks are basically giant holding tanks, each having a double set of gigantic metal gates on either end. The gates, ironically called leaves, weigh in at a staggering six hundred tons each with the largest ones, on the Pacific side of the canal, twenty-five metres high. Just one hinge on these enormous barriers weighs more than a double decker bus. After a vessel is guided into the lock by electric locomotives that run on tracks either side of the waterway, the leaves close and point upstream in a V shape, using water pressure to keep them closed. As I stood and looked on in amazement, giant valves opened and gravity forced water to flow into the lock from above, effortlessly raising a sixty thousand-ton super tanker almost nine metres above sea level. Once the water level in the two adjoining locks equalised, the front gates swung open and the vessel proceeded into the next lock, where the gates once again closed behind it and the process was repeated. It happened three times in total for a gain of twenty-six metres in altitude, using one hundred thousand cubic metres of water for each transit. To put it in perspective, that's enough water to fill forty Olympic sized swimming pools. On the Pacific side of the canal are another three locks although they are split into two sets. The single chambered Pedro Miguel Lock, lowers (or raises if you're coming from the opposite direction) nine and a half metres and two kilometres further down river the double Miraflores Locks lower a vessel the final sixteen and a half metres to a new ocean.

As impressive as the locks are they pale in comparison to the middle section of a vessel's journey through the Panama Canal through the Culebra Cut - formerly known as the Gaillard Cut - a 13 kilometre slice through the continental divide and one of the greatest feats of engineering this world has ever seen. Started by the French and finished by the Americans over a century ago, it's a marvel of man's persistence and ingenuity in the face of adversity. Tens of thousands of workers perished from malaria, yellow fever and other tropical diseases while undertaking to remove almost one hundred million cubic metres of rock as they blasted their way through the Culebra Mountain Range. From an initial sixty-four metres above sea level, The Cut snakes its way through the mountains at an altitude of twelve metres above sea level. Once the locks on both oceans were completed to a height of twenty-six metres, the space between them was flooded to create the Gatun Lake. The Culebra Cut filled with water and thus allowed vessels with a maximum draft (the length of a ship's keel under the water) of twelve metres to pass safely through a continent. A spectacular achievement any way you slice it!

A couple of days after our trip to the visitors' centre it was our turn to set off on one of the most memorable passages in any sailor's career. The fleet had already been split in two because not all thirty yachts could make the transit at the same time. Bobby, Stevie, Patrick and I fell in the second group aboard Free Spirit. Sheila's boat was in the first group so the previous day I'd waved her goodbye from the dock, hoping everything would run smoothly for both of us and we'd soon be reunited in Panama City.

Around midday, the fifteen yachts in our group set off together and headed to the 'flats,' a holding area where we waited for our advisor. It's obligatory for every non-commercial vessel to be accompanied by an advisor to ensure a safe transit. Ours, a short and rather rotund middle-aged Panamanian, arrived within the hour, sweating profusely. He was wearing a huge brimmed hat and every square inch of his body was covered in cloth except for the chubby circle of his podgy little face.

'Permission to come aboard,' he called out from the skiff that was depositing an advisor on each yacht.

'Permission granted,' acknowledged Bobby as the little chap heaved his way into the cockpit.

'Buenos días. ¿Cómo estás?' He asked with a smile that enveloped his entire round face.

'Bien gracias,' we replied.

'How are you this morning, Sir?' I asked in English, as the previous six words pretty much exhausted my entire Spanish vocabulary.

'I'm great thank you,' he reached for my hand and crushed it in a vice grip, 'I am Carlos.'

Soon after the pleasantries were exchanged, he spoke again.

'We have some time to wait before we head through the locks, would you happen to have something for me to eat and drink before we set off?'

Stevie popped below to prepare some refreshments and we quickly found out that Carlos's world revolved around his stomach and he attempted to eat us out of house and home. In-between scoffing whatever was put before him, our affable new companion told his story.

'My family have been working on this canal since its inception a century ago. I am the fifth generation to toil in the service of 'The Big Ditch.' My great, great grandfather helped to build it and the men in my family have been canal pilots ever since. I normally assist the big ships, but I love to pilot these little yachts too.'

'Little!' I exclaimed, feigning offence.

'Ha. I mean no insult! Fifty footers just feel small when you compare them to the thousand-foot Panamax vessels that come through.'

He grinned as he continued, 'later in the year the New Panamax locks open and they will be capable of taking twelve hundred footers.'

'Jesus,' I said, 'that's nearly as long as four football fields.'

'Yes, my friend. It is a whole lot of boat to manoeuvre with very little margin for error. This is why I occasionally like to help out with the smaller yachts. It's a very different experience seeing the locks from water level than from way up high on a cargo ship's bridge deck.'

Just then his walkie-talkie crackled into life and the command came through to get moving.

'Alright gentlemen, it is time to raft up with those two catamarans ahead of us. As we're a monohull, we get wedged in between the two others. Just think of them as two giant fenders protecting your yacht,' he added with a mischievous chuckle.

We motored alongside one of the catamarans and roped ourselves together, repeating the process as the second catamaran came alongside us, making us the ham in a big boat sandwich.

Carlos, as the most experienced pilot on either of the three boats, took command of our rather unwieldy raft. We slowly made our ponderous way towards the entrance of the first lock, surrounded by giant tankers and cargo ships crawling along in either direction, passing port side to port side, constrained by a set of imaginary lanes to prevent any head-on collisions.

It was finally our turn to enter the lock. The metal gates swung open like a giant set of jaws and admitted us into a dark and foreboding space. Surrounded by fifteen-metre-high crusty concrete walls lashed with giant scars from countless scrapes with the metal hulls of super tankers, it felt like we'd been swallowed into the belly of the beast as the barriers behind us clunked shut. As frigate birds swept overhead and the dock workers peered down from above I had the unnerving feeling of being penned in like a lamb to the slaughter. The sense of confinement was palpable as I felt the first twinge of claustrophobia I'd ever experienced on a boat.

I didn't have long to dwell on these thoughts as there was work to do. The minute we were positioned where Carlos wanted us, the call went out and the skyline filled with dock workers whirling ropes like slings, as if they were all little Davids about to take on a mighty Goliath. On the end of their lightweight lines was a tennis ball sized monkey fist knot which whizzed through the air at incredible speed before being released to fly in a perfect arc, landing with pinpoint accuracy on the deck of each outer yacht. As Free Spirit was in the middle of the pack, I was tasked to help out the yacht lashed to our starboard side. I caught the lightweight line thrown from above and attached it to one end of the inch-thick heavy duty, fifty metre warp we had collected in Shelter Bay before our departure. With one line fore and one line aft on either side of our raft, there were four in total. The light lines were hauled back ashore, dragging the heavy ropes behind them and made fast to bollards on the dock while we hooked the other end through a cleat on deck. A crew member standing at each corner of the raft took in the slack until all four ropes were taut, thus allowing us to maintain our position in the centre of the lock as the water came flooding in. So much water rushing into such a confined space created unpredictable currents and eddies. Our raft veered from left to right, but under the expert guidance of Carlos we took in the slack from each corner at varying speeds and stayed well clear of the unforgiving concrete that surrounded us. Imperceptibly at first, but with increasing speed, the water level crept up the walls of our enclosure and we began to rise out of the shadows and back towards the light. It was like an ascension towards heaven aboard a vertically moving yacht, a surreal experience indeed.

In less than ten minutes we were nine metres above sea level. After hauling the long warps back on board, the set of gates ahead of us swung open and beckoned us forth to repeat the same procedure two more times. In less than an hour, all fifteen yachts were safely through the Gatun Locks and the rafts disbanded to motor their way across Gatun Lake. Carlos directed us to the small boat mooring area where we stayed for the night, bidding us a fond farewell, but not before squaring away enough food to feed the Panamanian army.

Early the next morning Carlos bounded back on-board with his ever-present mischievous grin and his insatiable appetite and we set off for the Culebra Cut. For over two hours we motored through that incredible feat of engineering and the sheer scale of the project became apparent. The Cut wound its way through a path of the least amount of rocky resistance, but in some sections the topography of the land left the canal's surveyors no choice but to excavate straight through the middle of the mountains. At these points we were flanked by almost vertical, terraced cliff faces that rose fifty metres on either side, gouged out of the earth by the ingenuity of man. The extremely steep terraces require continuous maintenance to reduce the risk of landslides, but even so, the canal needs constant dredging to remain navigable. At an average of about two hundred metres wide the Cut was a phenomenal sight.

As I have found on many occasions in life, it's way easier to go downhill than it is to head uphill and the final three locks were no exception. On arrival we repeated the same process of rafting up and controlling our position with the four heavy duty lines sent ashore, but with the water draining out of the locks there was barely any turbulence at all. All we had to do was gradually release our lines and gravity did the rest. There was a little excitement in the last lock when I almost jumped for cover after what sounded like a gunshot. Seconds later the raft ahead of us slewed out of control and narrowly missed bouncing off the lock walls. We later found out that one of their crew members hadn't been concentrating, was too slow releasing their line and the immense pressure of tons of defending yacht ripped the cleat clean out of the deck. Besides that one little mishap, the rest of the yachts departed the final Miraflores Lock unscathed and entered the Pacific Ocean. As we sailed underneath the Bridge of the Americas connecting the north and south American land masses together, I felt a flush of pride. I'd just successfully transited one of the most iconic nautical milestones in the world, and before me stretched the vastest ocean on the planet. For the first time my dream of circumnavigating the globe began to feel like it might actually become a reality.

Chapter 5

Panama's Pearls

08°58'30N, 79°31'00W

On arrival in Panama I was greeted with a most welcome surprise. Sheila had left a message to meet up with her at the Hard Rock Hotel where she had booked a huge two room apartment with our friends, Stephen and Belle, an Australian couple who were also crewing on the World Arc. The idea was we'd easily be able to access Panama's Carnival that was just about to kick off and also enjoy some creature comforts and much needed privacy away from our respective boats.

As much as I love sailing, living on another person's yacht can be a trying ordeal at times. Some strange things happen when you are at sea for a long time and Bobby confirmed this fact. He started exhibiting a pathological hatred for any sand or saltwater on the boat, a rather peculiar perspective as those are two inescapable elements when sailing around the world.

Bobby made us shower after each dip in the water, clean anything that had been anywhere near the ocean - which was just about everything - and god forbid if a little salt water crept through an open hatch as that entailed a full fresh water wash down of the boat. It was good for everyone to get a little break from each other before tempers flared and I was happy to get away.

Panama City from our room in the Hard Rock Hotel

Our hotel room also had air conditioning, a king-sized double bed and limitless fresh water in a shower big enough to swing a cat in. It was extravagant, but the pure luxury after months of living in cramped conditions on a small boat was worth every cent.

It was also my first chance to experience an authentic Latin American Carnival and it was unlike anything I'd ever seen before. Carnival has its roots in a tradition of necessity dating back thousands of years.

At the end of winter in Europe's antiquity, villages held a feast to finish off all the food stocks left over in their larders that wouldn't survive the coming season. This feast was the last opportunity for common people to eat rich foods, like meat, before it spoilt in the warmer weather. It was the highlight of the year, a highly anticipated annual event in the run up to the lean months that followed before the next harvest.

As with all the pagan rites of the past, Christianity incorporated this tradition into its own calendar. *Carne vale,* or 'farewell to meat,' become its equivalent, followed by a period of religious abstinence preceding Easter - we know it as Lent. Over the past few centuries this festival has gradually been transformed from a religious observance into the modern-day excuse for one motherless party.

For four days the whole of Panama closes down and everybody lets loose, and when I say everybody, I mean everybody. There were little toddlers barely able to walk (a bit like their parents but for completely different reasons) to decrepit pensioners, sculling rum straight out of the bottle while drunken offspring pushed them around in their wheelchairs.

From noon until the sun rose the next morning the streets were awash with Panamanians eating, drinking, and doing their very best to get absolutely annihilated. *'Los Carnavales'* was debauchery on a country-wide scale, making it impossible not to get swept away by the sheer depravity of it all. The main party in Panama City centred around Avenida Balboa where the motorway was shut down and a huge section of it was fenced off to cage in all the revellers. The whole area was patrolled by a large military presence that attempted to keep a semblance of order.

Everyone was searched on the way into the compound to make sure that there were no concealed weapons but from then on it was a free for all that I dubbed 'Operation Obliteration'. Once we made it through security our senses were assaulted by the sights, sounds and smells. Songs were blaring out of speaker stacks whichever way I turned, with DJs competing to see who could produce the loudest and most distorted music. Just when I thought I might have found a little respite from the barrage of noise that was hammering my ear drums, another truck packed with rattling speakers rolled past to let me know what being loud really sounded like. Add to this a wild melee of humans in crazy costumes and various stages of undress, smoke from hundreds of barbecues and exploding fireworks, plus an icebox full of alcohol for sale situated every five paces and you start to get the idea of the level of carnage. Whenever the festivities started to quieten down a little, something new and dramatic happened. I'd be sampling the local delicacies from a vendor's stall when a horde of crazed lunatics in hideous devil costumes came screaming past, wailing like banshees and flailing each other with whips in a haunting parody of their enslaving Spanish ancestors or I'd be dancing in a mosh pit, bouncing off some beefy locals, when an outlandishly decorated fire truck rolled by, soaking all and sundry with its huge water cannons.

Each night culminated in a parade of exotic floats accompanied by marching bands and the ever-present beat of an African drum. I'm unsure if the word 'moderation' exists in the Spanish language, but there was certainly no evidence of it on display during Panama's Carnival. After four days of relentless partying it felt like my brain was bleeding through my battered ear drums and it was high time to return to the peace and tranquillity of the sea; my hedonistic desires well and truly sated for the time being.

It was time to say goodbye to the luxury of our en-suite room with its king-sized bed and giant bathroom. It was also time to say goodbye to Sheila as we took a taxi back to the port and went our separate ways, re-joining our respective crews but knowing we'd be together at the next anchorage.

Our next destination was the island of Contadora in the Las Perlas archipelago about thirty-five nautical miles offshore. Aptly named the Pearl Islands, these pristine little jewels, set in a mesmerising mantel of sapphire blue, were my first glimpse of the fabled Pacific islands I'd read so much about. For as long as I can remember I'd been devouring every bit of sailing literature I could get my hands on and reading about the Pacific always conjured up images of untouched islands with palm fronted white sandy beaches, beautiful blue expanses of sparkling water and exotic women.

Sheila and I met up and spent our days exploring the deserted beaches and rocky grottos that abounded on that little island paradise but there was only one noteworthy occurrence that profoundly affected the rest of my world trip. Tension had been building between Bobby and me for some time. On a personal level I liked the guy - he was intelligent, quirky and good value in a social environment. We'd enjoyed some great adventures together and I thought we'd forged a decent working relationship, but as a skipper I'd lost a lot of respect for him. To give him his due, he wasn't the worst skipper I had to endure on the trip, but then that's hardly high praise.

It all started at the Hotel Perla Real Beach Bar, a quaint little venue overlooking the anchorage where the fleet was moored. Sitting at a table surrounded by the rest of the crew Bobby asked, 'Daz, have you considered moving onto another yacht for a few of the next upcoming sailing legs?'

'Erm, no Bobby..., I haven't,' I replied, rather taken aback as his question came straight out of the blue. 'Why would I want to do that? I've committed to sailing with you until Australia.'

He took a drink from his glass and placed it on the table.

'I didn't mean as a permanent fixture. Rest assured, your berth on board Free Spirit is guaranteed, I just thought you might like a change of scenery for a while. You seem to be friends with everyone in the fleet so I'm sure it wouldn't be too difficult to arrange.'

At that point alarm bells started going off in my head. First of all, what a strange topic of conversation. Secondly, to broach the topic in front of the entire crew, instead of the private conversation it warranted, was wholly unprofessional.

I momentarily scrambled for the right words.

'I guess I can ask around,' I responded tersely as my hackles rose.

As far as I was concerned, Bobby and I had made a commitment to sail halfway around the world together. If there is only one thing you need to know about me, then that is if I say I'm going to do something, it gets done. My word is my bond and I will move heaven and earth to fulfil any promise I've made. For me, it's a question of personal integrity and family honour to be true to your word, but sadly this doesn't seem to hold true for everyone. My beer turned sour in the glass and I made my excuses to leave the table. Bobby had caught me totally unawares.

Sitting halfway down the beach I spotted my good friend and fellow fanatical fisherman, Massimo, and I went to ask for his opinion. Over a few more beers we discussed the matter and he came to the same conclusion as me. This was more than strange and didn't bode well for my future of sailing on Free Spirit.

I tried to put it to the back of my mind as I didn't want to think too much more about it, convincing myself there were important things to do like drink and have fun with my friends, but it soon become apparent that my days on Bobby's boat were drawing to a close.

The next day we planned a party on the beach which coincided with a dramatic change in the sea state. The water went from being as a flat as a pancake in the morning to a four-foot shore break by the afternoon as the swell from a distant storm rolled into the bay. This was epic news for Aussie Stephen and me as we'd found a little bodyboard washed up on the beach, and the two of us used it to charge into the breaking waves, to hilarious effect. It wasn't such good news for the score of inflatable tenders attempting a D-Day style landing on the beach in such horrendous conditions. With the understanding of wave patterns both Stephen and I had acquired from a lifetime of playing in the surf, we grabbed some volunteers and proceeded to do our civic duty. Over the next two hours we ran up and down the beach helping everyone ashore - from octogenarians to eight-year olds, everybody managed to get ashore safely. Over one hundred people ran the gauntlet and survived unscathed. All except one. In the headlong dash up the beach to get Free Spirit's tender above the waterline, Bobby stubbed his toe on a rock. The rest of the night was a blur of good-natured banter and endless alcohol as the whole fleet bought us round after round of drinks in thanks for our tireless work in getting them all safely ashore.

When I woke up the next morning, I was feeling a little fuzzy from the night's festivities, bruised and a little battered from the physical exertions of dragging thirty boats up the beach, but genuinely chuffed with myself for the help I'd given to everyone in the fleet. My positive outlook on the previous day's proceedings didn't last long as Bobby theatrically limped on deck and began to berate me for the excessive force I'd employed in shifting his tender.

'If you hadn't been running up the beach in such haste, if you'd been a little more thoughtful about those around you, I wouldn't be nursing a bloody broken toe, Daz!'

'You're joking right?'

'No, I'm not. You were pulling the tender too fast.'

'Jesus man, you have to be fast,' I said, 'otherwise you get caught in the breaking wave.'

He went on and on.

Man up you pansy, were the words that sprang to mind but I counted to three and managed to bite my tongue. In normal circumstances, if somebody blamed me for their own misfortune, especially for something as trivial as stubbing a toe, it would be laughable and immediately ridiculed with a comment along those lines.

Living and sailing on somebody else's yacht is far from normal, especially when you're faced with the irate owner of the vessel. To make my dream of sailing around the world a reality I needed Free Spirit, so I had to bite my tongue - considerably more challenging than it sounds as I could hear muffled giggling coming from the Stevie and Patrick, listening in from below decks. What little respect I had left for Bobby evaporated and I knew things would be changing soon. An uncertain and risky future beckoned but then, what else had I expected? It's been the common fate shared by sailors for millennia, so why would it be any different for me?

Chapter 6

The Galapagos

00°54'00S, 89°36'45W

It was an unexciting week's passage from Las Perlas to the Galapagos, but relations between Bobby and me were starting to feel rather strained. Everything he did was starting to piss me off and in hindsight I know I was subconsciously preparing myself to leave his boat. Although it was an uneventful sail, it was actually a huge benchmark for all aboard as we were about to cross the equator. There are a few recognised milestones in any sailor's career and crossing from one hemisphere into another for the first time is one of the major ones. It was the first time any of us had sailed across the equator and time to celebrate. For a true sailing circumnavigation, it's required to cross all three hundred and sixty meridians, plus the equator (at least once) and return to the original port you set off from without missing one nautical mile in between. Crossing the equator was the second major benchmark of my circumnavigation, the Panama Canal being the first.

Most seamen, when crossing the equator for the first time, undergo an initiation ceremony into the Kingdom of Neptune, transferring them from slimy pollywogs to trusty shellbacks. It's an old sailing tradition where the most experienced sailors aboard, and only those who have crossed the equator already, get in fancy dress and officiate over a farcical, kangaroo court where the inexperienced sailors' characters are judged.

Seeing that none of us had managed a line crossing before, I was happy to forego this ritual as there wasn't anybody on board worthy of holding court for the ceremony, but Bobby, not satisfied with crossing the line once, decided he'd zig-zag back and forth five times so he could brag to his friends he'd sailed across the equator multiple times.

For thousands of years, sailing has been an occupation of exploration, requiring a specific set of skills to survive, passed down from one generation to the next. Children as young as eight years old joined a ships company and began their training at the very bottom rung of the naval ladder - as cabin boys. They were taught how to work the ropes and sails, cook and clean and slowly assimilated the thousands of other skills required to survive safely on a boat. Only after decades of proficient service would the most capable individuals hope to summit the heady heights of becoming a ship's captain.

This legacy of nautical knowledge through experience still survives and is followed by any sailor with a shred of common sense. But sadly, these days it is no longer a prerequisite for sailing. Now, anybody with enough money can go and buy a boat, put on a cap, call themselves a skipper and head straight out to sea with minimal experience. Armed only with an inflated sense of self-importance and a big ego a skipper will soon get a good battering from the ocean.

As we crisscrossed the equator, I could have thrown Bobby overboard as he behaved more like a tourist than an ocean skipper, unwittingly demeaning one of the most important rites of passage for any seaman.

As we neared our destination, I had a mounting sense of excitement and I made up my mind that Bobby wasn't going to spoil it. I'd wanted to explore the Galápagos Islands from the second I'd read about them in a well-thumbed copy of The National Geographic I'd scavenged from my uncle Gordon's library when I was ten years old.

Not only are the islands teeming with species of flora and fauna found nowhere else on earth, they also helped to change mankind's view of his place in the world.

In 1835, aboard HMS Beagle, a young naturalist called Charles Darwin voyaged to the Galápagos. After observing the beaks of hundreds of similar sized finches, he noticed a marked variation in the shapes of the birds' beaks. The structure, it appeared, was dependent on what the birds ate on the different islands in the archipelago. Those observations planted a seed in his mind that would grow into an idea, that when published more than twenty years later, would cause one of the greatest upheavals in the history of the natural sciences. The fabled isles we were heading to were the birthplace of Darwin's theory of evolution by natural selection, and for me, the home of natural history as we know it. After a quarter of a century of dreaming about exploring the Galápagos I was about to get the chance, and if what we witnessed on our arrival was anything to go by, then there was no way it was going to be a disappointment.

In the last five miles, as we sailed towards San Cristobal, I saw more wildlife in an hour than I'd seen in the last month. There were immense flocks of boobies and frigate birds, sharks, giant turtles and barking sea lions. Manta rays breached the surface, flying straight out of the water and up into the air before crashing back down with mighty splashes. It seemed as if the entire ecosystem made an effort to head out and welcome us in. I couldn't wait to get ashore after such a spectacular natural reception no other islands have even come close to eclipsing, but I was to be disappointed.

The Ecuadorian Government's entry formalities into the Galápagos took bureaucracy to a whole new level and the whole of the first day was spent waiting for representatives from customs and immigration, the parks board and quarantine. We had fifteen people in three different parties come aboard to check all was in order. Scuba divers searched our hull for any foreign crustaceans. Because we'd travelled from the Atlantic Ocean, through the Panama Canal and into the Pacific Ocean, the Galápagos authorities didn't want any cross contamination of species from two different oceans. It was frustrating but wholly necessary. Unfortunately, a Finnish Boat in our fleet was sent forty miles offshore with a diver on board to scrape off the seven barnacles found attached to their hull, a costly and wasteful day easily avoided with a quick scrape in Las Perlas.

It may sound pedantic to be this over-protective, but the habitats found in the Galápagos are unparalleled anywhere else in the world. They need to be vigorously protected to allow future generations to marvel at their splendour so I cannot fault the island's administrators for their dedication.

Sea lions lounge wherever they please in the Galápagos

The next morning after all the formalities were concluded it was finally time to explore. The first thing I noticed when heading ashore was the large quantity of enormous sea lions sprawled on every available surface and it quickly became apparent that they couldn't have cared less that I was there. While they lounged at full stretch in the sun, I literally tripped over them as I made my way along the sea wall. God forbid I wanted to sit on one of the promenade's benches and rest for a minute in the stifling forty-degree heat because in seconds, one of those lumbering giants would amble over and dissuade me from such a foolish notion. I didn't want to be crushed by two hundred kilograms of smelly blubber, so it was definitely in my best interest to get out of their way. This general disdain for humans wasn't unique to the sea lions though. Creatures both great and small displayed absolutely no fear of people, to the point where I'd finally found a quiet spot in the shade just to chill out and take it all in, when a juvenile lava lizard ran up my arm. I must have looked more interesting than the boulder he was warming up on as he perched disdainfully on my forearm, looking up at me as if to say, 'who are you and what do you think you're doing sitting on one of my rocks?'

It struck me that the Galápagos Islands are what the world must have been like before man came along and fucked it all up.

The next creature I saw was casually strolling down the promenade as if it owned the place. With ragged claws, dark piercing eyes and a scaly hide full of spikes came the prehistoric looking marine iguana. This endemic (only found in the Galápagos) species is unique among lizards as it's the only one that forages for algae from the ocean and is capable of diving to depths of over twenty metres for up to an hour. It was extraordinary to watch those little dinosaurs mechanically plod their way down the beach, and after a cold reptilian stare, sprint the last few metres into the ocean, propelling themselves through the surf with their flattened tails before disappearing from sight as they dove to the ocean floor.

This reptile is so well adapted to its environment that it's developed a gland in its nose which removes excess salt from its body. I saw hundreds of them perched on the black volcanic rocks, warming themselves up after a swim in the icy waters, squirting away their unwanted detritus in powerful snot rockets, but they have an even more impressive talent. There is a cyclical phenomenon called El Niño which brings warmer water to the ocean's surface. In the years when it occurs the warm layer reduces the upwelling from the depths of the cold, nutrient rich waters that feed the Galápagos. This results in a decrease in available phytoplankton, the primary building block of the ocean's food chain, creating a knock-on effect for all the predators further up the ladder as food resources become limited and many leave, if they can, or face starvation. The red algae that marine iguanas rely on for survival is unproductive in these conditions and an indigestible invasive brown alga takes over. With no escape from the islands, and no available food source, up to ninety percent of the marine iguana population can perish, but miraculously they still manage to cling to life in the most incredible fashion. Unlike any other vertebrates, marine iguanas evolved an ability to shrink themselves when times are tough. By reabsorbing their own skeletons, they can make enough energy available to survive in one of the harshest environments on earth, making them, in my opinion, the coolest reptiles on the planet.

After I spent hours exploring the immediate vicinity in the blistering heat it was time to call it a day and head to one of the local bars. I caught up with my mates from other yachts in the fleet and we all hoisted a pint or three in celebration of arriving somewhere that most of us had only ever dreamt of. It was a great night and we celebrated in style.

The next morning, I woke to a pungent odour permeating my cabin and it turned out a sea lion's favourite lounging location isn't a public bench. Why should they go to all the effort of waddling ashore when there were perfectly serviceable yachts to climb onto? I doubt there are many occasions in life that make you feel quite as useless as I did that morning. Dressed only in my boxer shorts and armed with a broom, I had to prod away at three massive beasts snapping at me as I attempted to shoo them out of the cockpit. They were three times my size and pretty pissed off at being poked with a stick. After lots of shouting and jostling from me, they eventually gave in and dove into the water, but not before giving me a last scouring red eyed stare and an abusive bark over their shoulders.

The only solution to this rather large problem was to barricade the swimming platform with all our fenders – the inflatable bumpers used to stop the hull from getting scratched when docking - so the sea lions couldn't climb onto the boat. It just about managed to do the trick, but it was a war of attrition and in any siege there are always casualties, as one of our trusty fenders found out. It paid the ultimate price, exploding under the gargantuan bulk of a particularly determined sea lion while valiantly attempting to repulse the illegal squatter.

As cool as the marine iguanas were, they do have some competition if they want to claim the title of top reptile of the Galapagos. Step forward, albeit slowly, the giant tortoise. These immense creatures grow in excess of four hundred kilograms and have a life expectancy of over a century. Named '*Insulae de los*

Galapegos' by the first sailors that arrived there, the Islands of the Tortoises were once home to a quarter of a million of these lumbering giants. They are incredible creatures capable of surviving for up to a year without food or water, and this made them an ideal long-term fresh food source for nautical voyages. Sadly, the very characteristics that evolved over millions of years to enable them to survive in their harsh environment were the same ones that nearly lead to their extinction. Ruthlessly exploited by the earliest mariners, the population was decimated and a third of the fifteen species that were once abundant on the islands are now extinct. The population was down to a minuscule three thousand in the 1970's but through tenacious conservation and breeding programmes, their numbers have bounced back, but it's heart-breaking to think just how close mankind came to annihilating these regal reptiles.

Five of the nineteen islands are inhabited with a combined permanent population of around 25,000 people. The regulations on the islands are so tight that once you are out of the main towns, all travel is strictly monitored. You couldn't go anywhere without a guide and I found this quite difficult to get used to as there's nothing I love more than to go exploring on solo adventures, far from the madding crowd. It was not the end of the world though as I developed a cunning tactic for peeling off the back of my tour group. I let the rest of them forge ahead and then dawdled along, quietly taking in the surroundings on my own from the relative peace and quiet of the rear and this practice initially irritated the guides. They politely reprimanded me several times, until they realised I knew enough about the flora, fauna and conservation not to cause any damage and left me in peace. Being shown five different types of endemic moss didn't really tickle my fancy so I was more than happy to amble along, in absolute awe, as I made my own discoveries along the way.

Lost in my own thoughts on one of these hikes it came as quite a surprise that it had never occurred to me how barren a volcanic island could look. Whenever I thought of the South Pacific, it always conjured up images of palm trees and lush vegetation. This may be true for the islands lying further to the west, but as I'm sure you've worked out by now, the Galápagos are different. As we trekked towards the northern tip of San Cristobal and up into the mountains, the vegetation all but disappeared with only a few scattered cacti and hardy shrubs left. From exploring the relatively fertile lowlands in the south where frigate birds swooped on a freshwater lake to clean their salty feathers, to hiking at altitude through a desert with only a few scattered boobies' nests, the contrast couldn't have been more pronounced. There is no wonder that the Galápagos is home to such a range of diverse species found nowhere else on earth.

San Cristobal island's most iconic landmark, Kicker Rock, is situated a couple of nautical miles offshore. It is the remnants of an old lava cone that split in two and the diving there is spectacular. Galápagos sharks, turtles and vast arrays of schooling fish where pretty standard sights, but I went specifically to catch sight of one of the strangest looking fish in the ocean - the scalloped hammerhead shark.

Using their elongated heads like metal detectors, these alien looking creatures sweep the ocean floor. Their senses are so finely tuned that they are capable of detecting the minute electromagnetic signals given off by their prey before they pounce with breath-taking speed and agility. Occasionally, the hammerheads cruise in huge schools, hundreds strong, but I was just as thrilled to catch my first sighting of a solitary shark as it came cruising by. With its head swaying from side to side and eyes set far apart, it was capable of seeing both above and below itself at all times, a ferocious predator ceaselessly scanning the ocean for food. Hammerheads eat a vast array of prey from fish - including other sharks - to cephalopods and crustaceans, but their favourite food is stingray.

When we returned to the surface there was more drama when we witnessed Darwin's theory of natural selection and the survival of the fittest. As we sat in the dive boat discussing our hammerhead sighting, something caught my eye. Plummeting from the heights of Kicker Rock above us came a shrieking little fluffy white ball of down feathers that hit the water with an audible splash. A juvenile booby had fallen from its nest over a hundred metres above, perhaps an accident or a deliberate push from a stronger sibling as they competed for food. It was heart breaking to hear its distressed calls as it bobbed helplessly on the water's surface. We all watched on as our guides explained they couldn't interfere with this natural process and the little guy's fate was already sealed. The last we saw of him was from a distance as the frigate birds, spotting a defenceless meal, began their aerial bombardment. It was a poignant reminder of how tenuous life can be.

The rest of the afternoon Sheila and I spent exploring a deserted white sandy cove. The charmingly named Sally Lightfoot crabs - said to be named after a Caribbean dancer light on her feet - scurried before us in their technicolour dream coats as we explored the shoreline.

The ever-present sea lions frolicked on the beach as marine iguanas baked themselves in the sun while a multitude of sea birds soared in the sky and pelicans plunged headlong into the surf. Reef sharks and stingrays leisurely patrolled the coastline and the occasional turtle popped up for air. While I sat on that beach, completely surrounded by nature's beauty, a feeling of complete harmony swept over me. This was how the world was meant to be and I felt incredibly privileged to be a part of it.

Our next port of call was the island of Isabella and the overnight sail there was the most surreal passage of my entire circumnavigation. I'd never before experienced an ocean devoid of any motion whatsoever. With absolutely zero wind or swell, it was so flat there was a mirror image of the cloudless sky in the water, and the whole solar system was perfectly reflected on the ocean's shining surface. To be completely surrounded by twinkling stars felt more like I was an astronaut in a spacecraft than a sailor aboard a ship, flying my way towards the next destination instead of floating there. If it wasn't for the ripple of our wake astern, I'd have been convinced I was in another dimension.

Isabella is the biggest island in the archipelago and it's roughly shaped like a giant seahorse. Comprising of six volcanoes, five of which are still active, it is one of the most volcanic places on earth. As part of my birthday celebrations, Sheila and I booked a tour to 'Los Tuneles' on the south coast. When a volcano erupts, molten lava flows downhill, occasionally forming lava tubes when the exterior layer of liquid rock solidifies first, while the lava inside continues to flow and underground tunnels are created. After millions of years of erosion from the relentless motion of the ocean an incredible labyrinth of bridges, arches and caves has formed. It is a veritable playground for the abundant sea life that call it home.

The snorkelling was incredible and we swam with the biggest turtles I'd ever seen. Those giant green turtles weighed in at a staggering three hundred kilograms and were one and a half metres long. Docile in nature, they rested on the sea floor, munching their way through the prolific beds of sea grass. Once they'd hoovered up one patch they'd glide onto the next. It never ceases to amaze me how effortlessly such large creatures can move through the water. I even dove with one individual who was missing a rear fin, most likely the result of a shark attack, who displayed no less speed or agility than the rest. The treat of the day came when I bumped into a little bird you'd never expect to find there. At fifty centimetres tall and two and a half kilograms in weight, the Galápagos Penguin is the second smallest penguin in the world and the only species of its kind to live naturally in the Northern Hemisphere. Swathed in black feathers with a smattering of white and grey marks on their faces, beaks and chests, they're the cutest little critters you'll ever see, standing hunched over as they slowly shuffle around to keep their sensitive feet from getting sunburnt.

Our day's diving was complete when our guide spotted a beautiful little sea horse nestled in the rocks. It was so well camouflaged that it took me half a dozen dives before I caught sight of it. I love those little creatures and it's always a special day for me when I see one on a dive, especially when they're the same shape as the magical island I'm diving off.

There were only two creatures left that I wanted to see, the Blue Footed Booby and the Flightless Cormorant. The former is pretty abundant if you know where to look, the latter has a far more restricted range of only two islands, making them difficult to find in just a few inaccessible spots. You have to love the Blue Footed Booby, not only for its comical name (it originally comes from the Spanish word '*bobo*' meaning silly or stupid) but for the ungainly walk they exhibit on land, slapping down their big blue clown shoes as they waddle along, staring at you with the most piercing yellow eyes. Their feet are coloured a bright blue by the pigments they ingest from their diet of fresh fish. These pigments act as antioxidants, bolstering their immune systems and the brighter the feet, the healthier the bird, and the healthier the bird the more sexually attractive they appear to prospective mates.

I didn't manage to see any of the flightless cormorants in the end, but that's a good thing. I've got a good reason to return one day, not that I'd ever need an excuse to head back to those enchanted isles.

Unfortunately, our cruising permit was only for a fortnight and only allowed us access to the three main islands. So, it was time to depart and wave goodbye to one of the most unique islands on earth. We were the last yacht to pull anchor from Isabella's harbour, which turned out to be very fortunate for another boat in our fleet. Giampi, owned by my buddy Massimo, had barely made it a mile out to sea before experiencing engine troubles. With no wind and no power, this could have posed a serious issue, but fortunately we were on hand to tow them to Santa Cruz. This earned us numerous bottles of wine from Massimo's seemingly inexhaustible supply and it helped to cement a friendship that would later prove to be crucial for my future circumnavigation success. Fortunately for Massimo, the problem was pretty simple to solve. A large squid had been sucked up through the cooling system, blocking the water intake and overheating his engine.

Santa Cruz was the most built up and busiest of the islands we visited. There were still plenty of interesting animals around, but it had a much more commercial feel about it. The scuba diving off North Seymour was amazing and seeing flocks of flamingos on an island in the middle of the ocean seemed pretty surreal, but sadly I had a much more pressing matter to concern myself with.

Bobby had finally worked up the courage to tell me he'd decided to keep the newest member of the crew, Stevie, instead of me. He made the excuse that having a good chef on board was the reason he'd decided to let me go. In fairness, he'd always alluded to the idea of shortening the crew for cruising in French Polynesia but my place to Australia was meant to be assured. I was incredibly disappointed in him for breaking his word, but we still had a three thousand nautical mile ocean crossing ahead of us so I had to make the best of it.

I discussed the matter with Massimo, my trusted advisor and a sailor for whom I had the upmost respect.

'Bad news buddy, I'm off the boat.'

'Ah, sorry my friend,' Massimo replied, 'if I had space on Giampi you would join us. Sadly, I'm full until Tonga, but when you make it that far then I promise there is a guaranteed place for you.'

'Cheers buddy, I might take you up on that offer, but first I've got to get there.'

'Do you need to change boats immediately?'

'Nah,' I replied, 'Bobby hasn't been a total wanker and left me completely high and dry. I still have my ocean passage across the Pacific to the Marquesas, so I've got some time.'

'What reason did he give for wanting you off his boat?' Massimo enquired.

'Some garbled bollocks about wanting a chef and a quieter boat, whatever that means.'

He burst out laughing, 'That's pretty funny Daz!'

I looked at him confused, 'Why is it?'

'He does have a point. You're certainly not the most reserved sailor I've ever met. You're a character, Daz, and that's the underlying problem. You're stealing his limelight.'

'Nah, I'm not.'

'Yes, you are! Most people associate Free Spirit with you, not Bobby, and he doesn't like it.'

I shook my head in disbelief as he continued.

'And I bet he's had just about enough of you questioning all of his sailing decisions. No skipper likes to be undermined on his own boat.'

'I only question his stupid decisions.'

'You're probably right most of the time too, but I bet he feels rather intimidated by you.'

'But I can't stand by and keep my mouth shut when somebody is about to do something stupid and endanger the crew's safety.'

Massimo raised an eyebrow, 'you still have much to learn about people, my friend.'

He passed me another beer, 'but that is a chat for another day. Let us solve one problem at a time. What are you going to do?'

'Well, I've asked around and all the other yachts in the fleet are full, bar one.'

'Let me guess, Harry on Wanderlust has lost another crew member,' he remarked with a chuckle.

'Yip, another one bites the dust,' I said, 'that many crew changes don't make for a happy ship, and his boat seems to be under constant running repairs. On the last leg they hit something underwater and lost a rudder. It seems like an unlucky yacht to me.'

'Yes, he has certainly had some bad luck and a Bavaria is not the yacht I would choose to cross any ocean with. Harry has managed to fix everything that has broken on his boat himself, including replacing the rudder. He's got much further than I'd ever have thought possible for someone of his limited sailing experience. I'm sure he could do with your help.'

Massimo and I continued to mull it over and we came to the conclusion that if Harry and Wanderlust managed to complete the next section across the Pacific safely (the longest ocean passage in the world), then I would surely survive some island hopping until I made it as far as Tonga, where I could move onto Giampi. Little did I know at the time how instrumental I'd be in Wanderlust's future survival. With my future progress temporarily taken care of, it was time to get back to work and make the final preparations aboard Free Spirit for the mammoth three week crossing ahead.

Chapter 7

A time of reflection

06°S,115°W

Open Google Earth spin it to the side where the Pacific Ocean is situated and take a look at what you see. That's right, almost one entire half of our globe is blue except for the occasional splash of green from a few isolated islands. It is so immense you can fit the area of all the land masses on our planet into it and still have enough space left over to squeeze in another six Mediterranean Seas!

The Pacific is by far the largest ocean on our little orb and its enormity has always been a daunting prospect for any mariner attempting to cross it. These huge distances only exacerbate the many difficulties faced by sailors in their quest to survive the savage seas. The biggest hurdle for sailors has always been water. I'm not talking about the salty water you float on, although that provides challenge enough, but the fresh water you need just to survive. Humans can do without food for almost a month, but without drinking water in the equatorial heat you wouldn't last a week. On board Free Spirit we had two 300 litre water tanks, separated from each other to ensure there wouldn't be a total loss of water supply if one of them became contaminated or sprung a leak. In total, that's equivalent to how much water you'd use to run seven baths. It's not a lot when you consider the water needed for cooking, drinking and cleaning for four men over a three-week voyage.

But man has always been an innovative little beast, bent on problem solving, and has invented some incredible gadgets. High up on that list has to be the reverse osmosis water maker. Simply put, saltwater is forced under high pressure through a semi-permeable membrane. This membrane allows the small water molecules to pass through, but not the larger salt ones and 'voila', you can turn the ocean's brine into delicious fresh drinking water. With one of these magical machines on board we were able to replenish our water levels, allowing us to have a shower every day, albeit for only a minute. A one-minute shower may sound like a trivial thing, but on smaller boats without water making facilities, you only get about half a litre of water a day for your ablutions. So being able to take a quick shower before heading to bed every night is the equivalent of five-star luxury and it makes a long voyage infinitely more endurable.

Food is the next most important thing on a boat. On a passage across the Pacific on a yacht the size of Free Spirit, it is necessary to plan for a month's meals. The extra week is a safety margin in case of any emergency that may prolong the voyage. That's twenty-eight breakfasts, lunches and dinners for four people, a total of three hundred-and-thirty-six meals. The range of products most of us take for granted in our huge supermarkets at home aren't available around the world, which adds to the challenge. Unless you want to eat the same thing day in day out, it takes considerable ingenuity to maintain a healthy and varied diet. Fresh fruit and vegetables only last about ten days at sea, so this also needs to be considered and supplemented with tinned goods that do not spoil. Catching fresh fish - my speciality - is an added bonus but by no means guaranteed.

Cooking aboard most vessels is generally shared equally by the members of the crew unless you have a professional chef on board. We didn't, so each of us took it in turns to prepare breakfast lunch and dinner every fourth day. These mealtimes become the focal point of your day and help to establish a solid routine at sea. It's really the only time when the whole ship's company gets a chance to sit down together, and a good-natured rivalry develops between the competing *chefs*. I've sailed with people who could burn water, but generally everybody pitches in and tries their best, and it all adds to the unique experience that is long distance sailing.

Once all the logistical issues are sorted, there is no greater feeling of freedom than setting out on an ocean voyage. The second you hoist your anchor all your worldly problems cease to exist. You become a totally self-sufficient entity with everything you need to survive on board. Any difficulties that arise have to be dealt with under your own steam as there is no external help available. It's just you, the crew and your yacht. Within a few hours you lose sight of the land, and then it is just blue water for as far as the eye can see. Once you're totally surrounded by three hundred and sixty degrees of unforgiving ocean you must become fully immersed in your new environment if you wish to survive one of the most hostile places under the sun.

Whenever I set off on a long ocean crossing, I never know what the future may bring. A shiver of excitement always runs down my spine as I look towards the horizon and wonder what's out there. Rain or shine, all the external factors are out of my control and I let go of everything except the here and now. Come what may, I have to forge ahead and survive the elements and it is the most liberating feelings I've ever experienced. I believe this is the way we were all born to live our lives, destined to explore and marvel at our beautiful planet. To wake up each and every day excited about the exhilarating challenges that lie ahead. Humans aren't born to sit in offices and watch their lives slowly tick away, minute by minute, counting down the days until their next holiday. I've been there, trying to earn enough money to fund my next adventure, watching other colleagues working year after year, earning more and more money to buy mass produced rubbish they don't even need; an endless cycle of consumption to stave off the boredom of unfulfilling lives.

Sailing is an opportunity to reconnect with the basic components that make us human. Everything boils down to the simple ingredients of life as the superficial clutter we surround ourselves with in the modern world fades away. There are no social media notifications pinging on your phone or the pointless emails your boss expects to be answered immediately. There is just the mesmerising blanket of blue-sky overhead and the carpet of sapphire water below. It is a humbling experience when you realise just how insignificant all that bollocks really is. At sea you simply exist in the present moment and are happy to be alive, re-energised by the stark beauty of the incredible planet we are so fortunate to call home.

As we headed south from the Galapagos we encountered the Intertropical Convergence Zone (ITCZ), an area of low pressure found in a band around the equator. The ITCZ is situated between the trade wind system of the two hemispheres and is an area of variable wind conditions. Commonly referred to by mariners as the Doldrums, it has becalmed sailing vessels for weeks at a time in its dull and listless clutches. There is nothing more frustrating in sailing than being becalmed. With no forward momentum for stability you are rocked from side to side by the ocean's swell, comparable to sitting on a giant rocking horse. Add to this horrible motion the constant banging of the rigging and the relentless groaning of the hull, all the while being stuck in a confined space where there is nowhere to hide, no escape, and with no idea how long the lack of wind is going to last. It drives me crazy after only a couple of hours of this torture so I cannot imagine what it must have felt like for the sailors of yesteryear who endured that madness for weeks on end. Fortunately, we had an engine, so once the wind disappeared, we fired up the iron spinnaker and motored due south for a couple of days, quickly escaping the clutches of that forlorn and windless zone.

Three weeks at sea may sound like an incredibly long time but it flies by. The general daily routine of cooking, cleaning and covering your watches gets your mind and body into a rhythm. As long as you keep a vigilant look out for other vessels during your watch you have ample time for enjoying the simple things in life like reading, fishing and just kicking back on the long ocean swell. Talking of fish, one monster from the depths sounded the death knell for the last shred of respect I had for Bobby.

In the first fortnight of the journey I'd barely touched a fish, even though I'd fished from the second the sun rose to when it set twelve hours later. Through the Doldrums I hadn't even hooked a fish for seven days. I'd only landed a couple afterwards that were so small it was a shame to take them away from their mum, so I'd let them go. Since setting out from Las Palmas all I'd wanted was to land one monster, just one big game fish I could have a proper battle with and feed the whole crew. I thought my time had come when one morning, while staring over the stern at my favourite pink lure trailing behind, a tuna in excess of fifty kilograms and the size of a torpedo, burst forth from the depths and hammered my line with the force of a freight train.

'FISH! FISH! FISH!' I shouted, frantically grabbing my rod with its screaming reel as the tuna dove at full speed to allude capture.

Within seconds Stevie was in the cockpit and on hand to help.

'What can I do, bro?'

'You've got to stop the fucking boat man, this is monstrous, where's Bobby? Quick, get Bobby!'

It takes two people to drop the spinnaker, the big billowing sail that flies from the bow of the boat.

'Bobby! Bobby! FISH!' I screamed at the top of my voice.

All the while my line was streaming out. One hundred metres, a hundred-and-fifty, there was no let up and still no Bobby.

Stevie was shouting too; he knew how wonderful it would be for the morale of the crew to put some freshly baked tuna on the dinner table. 'Bobby, where the hell are you?'

I pulled the rod up to my collar bone and tried to reel in. It was impossible, I couldn't fight the boat and the fish at the same time as more line streamed out.

'For fuck's sake Bobby, quick man.'

Just then he casually strolled on deck, ever so slowly putting on his gloves and began to make preparations for dropping the sail. In the past, with an incoming squall, we'd dropped that sail in two minutes flat and I couldn't believe it was taking so long. Minutes had already passed since I'd first called him and my shout is as loud as a foghorn.

I'd managed to slow the fish down, but I was running out of line.

'God damn it Bobby, slow the boat down,' I screamed in anguish.

I looked over my shoulder at Bobby. He was still fiddling with a finger of his glove.

'Hurry up I'm going to lose…'

As the words tumbled from my mouth there was a loud twang, my rod hit me in the side of the head, and I fell backwards. My line had snapped from the huge pressure it was under after dragging fifty kilos of raging flesh behind a boat still travelling at seven knots.

Heartbroken, I looked up in complete bewilderment from my stripped and smoking reel to see a strange smirk on Bobby's face.

'Oh well, I guess that one got away,' he said.

After sailing with him for such a long time he knew exactly what it meant for me to catch a game fish and in his own spiteful, pathetic little way he'd shown me he was still in charge of the boat.

I'm not proud to admit this but that was the one and only time on the entire trip that I had a tantrum. I flung my hat off in anger, slammed my rod and reel into the teak deck (chipping one of the planks in the process), and levelled such a baleful glare at Bobby that he went white. I was close to letting all my frustrations boil over as I felt the red mist begin to descend. It took all of my will power to control my rage as I barged past him and headed to my bunk to cool my temper. We still had a week to sail together, so I had to remain civil, but Bobby knew he'd overstepped the bounds of our relationship and I'd lost all respect for him as a man.

That evening, I dismantled my rod, unclipped the reel and packed all my fishing gear away. It would be some time before it saw the light of day again.

Free Spirit was equipped with an electric autopilot, a marvellous invention which freed up most of my time on watch as hand steering was only necessary in hazardous situations. Occasionally I had to make a sail change, or put in a reef or two, but generally speaking, once my boat duties were complete the rest of the time was mine. With so much free time, I spent my days refining my celestial navigation skills. Before the advent of Global Positioning Satellites (GPS), sailors had to navigate using the stars. Mathematicians used trigonometry to calculate the positions of the most prominent celestial bodies and collated their results in the Nautical Almanac. With a chronometer, a sextant and the almanac you can - with a little practice - work out your latitude and longitude anywhere on the globe to within a couple of nautical miles.

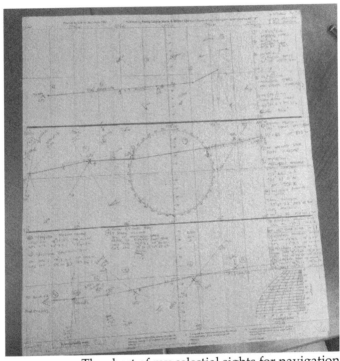

The chart of my celestial sights for navigation

Over the course of the journey I woke up every morning an hour before sunrise and took twilight star sights with the boat's sextant. In each quadrant of the sky, I found stars or planets still bright enough to see as the horizon appeared with the dawning of the day. Using the sextant, I measured the angle these stars or planets were above the horizon and noted the exact time, to the second, when I took the sight. I then plugged the information into an algorithm with values calculated from the sight reduction tables (just a fancy word for lots of numbers in the Almanac), and where these calculated lines intersected was where our boat should be.

It seemed like a very daunting and mystical process at first, but like almost everything else in life, once I gave it a go it wasn't that difficult and I wondered what all the fuss was about.

I repeated the process at sunset, waiting for the stars to appear before the horizon was totally obscured by darkness. I also took a Meridian Sight around noon each day to work out the exact Greenwich Mean Time when the sun was directly overhead – one needs to know GMT to work the chronometer. These different sights allow me to fix my latitude and longitude accurately on the huge, featureless ocean. This may sound like loads of work but nothing beats the feeling of security and accomplishment you get from knowing that, if all your electronic navigation systems fail, at least you'll know where you are on the ocean and be capable of navigating yourself to the next safe port of call.

From the practical side to a more spiritual one, all the star gazing immerses you in the cosmos. With daily practice you start to recognise the stars, planets and constellations as you track them across the sky. With no light pollution the stars are dazzling, and each night you get to contemplate your place in the universe. To put it in perspective, you can only see about five to six thousand stars with the naked eye and only about half of those at any one time due to the spherical shape of earth. The furthest of these visible stars is around a thousand light years away. With light travelling at 300,000km/s, a thousand light years is a seriously long distance.

In our galaxy, the Milky Way, there are about two hundred and fifty billion stars, and there is an estimated hundred billion galaxies in our universe. So, there's an unfathomable number of stars out there, and we don't even live on a star, but on one of the eight planets that orbit our star - the Sun - in this tiny little solar system we call home. Out in the middle of the world's biggest ocean, staring towards the heavens and surrounded by the brightest stars imaginable really starts to give you an idea how infinitesimally small you are and how brief your allotted time on earth is. All the more justification to follow your dreams, as time is short, and ours will all be over in the blink of a cosmic eye.

Chapter 8

Paradise on earth

09°48'15S, 139°02'30W

It was impossible to contain my excitement as I shouted with glee, 'Land ho!'

It had been a very long three-week crossing, and I was ecstatic to see my old friend terra firma again. Unlike jet-setting on an aeroplane, where you can be anywhere in the world within twenty-four hours, a long-haul ocean crossing on a yacht intensifies your anticipation of every arrival at a new destination. All the time and energy spent getting yourself there gives you the feeling that you've earned the privilege of accessing the remote islands you visit.

Hiva Oa is an island in the Marquesas Archipelago and was our first port of call in French Polynesia. It's an unbelievably lush green island rearing straight out of the ocean. Standing at an impressive twelve hundred metres above sea level, it came as quite a shock to the senses after the endless blue of the sky and ocean.

We headed straight for Taha Uku, a little harbour next to Atuona Bay and the only safe anchorage on the island. A little sea wall has been built to provide some protection from the ocean's swell but the majority of the fleet had already anchored behind it so it was a challenge to find a space big enough for us to drop our hook.

After a couple of unsuccessful attempts, we finally found some good holding and dug the anchor in. If the wind were to shift in such close quarters, boats would bounce off each other, so it was imperative for us also to lay a stern anchor. Playing dodgems with other people's yachts isn't a good way to make new friends as someone in the fleet was soon to find out.

With the boat safely anchored fore and aft, we made our way ashore to check in with the French Bureaucracy and to reacquaint ourselves with our cruising friends, most of whom we'd not seen in a month. Sheila, sporting a flower garland and looking radiant with her dark tan contrasting beautifully with her halo of blond hair gave me a big hug on the dock and thrust something into my hand.

'Eat that,' she said with a smile, 'you'll never have tasted anything like it.'

I laughed at her, 'Oi, I've only been ashore less than five minutes and you're already telling me what to do.'

I took it from her. 'What is it?'

'Pamplemousse, it's just about the sweetest and most delicious thing on the island,' she poked me in the stomach, 'except for me of course.'

She was right, as usual. It looked like a common pink grapefruit but tasted so different. Instead of the sour juice I was expecting, that little beauty's sweet nectar seemed like a gift straight from the gods - like biting into pure sunshine.

After a fortnight without fresh fruit my taste buds were in ecstasy as I attacked the fruit with relish. Just thinking about the natural, sugary goodness dripping down my chin still makes me salivate and recall that wonderful moment, spent sitting in the sun with a beautiful girl by my side, on my first pacific island in French Polynesia. I was infused with a great sense of achievement having successfully sailed across the greatest expanse of unbroken ocean in the world.

After being cooped up for such a long voyage there was nothing for it but to stretch my legs and go for a walk into the main town.

The humidity was brutal and both Sheila and I were a sweaty mess by the time we arrived in Atuona an hour later, wilting in the tropical heat. The island of Hiva Oa is most famous for being the final resting place of Paul Gauguin, the French post-Impressionist painter who decided to escape civilisation in an attempt to remain true to his more primitive form of artistic expression. He settled on the island at the beginning of the twentieth century, but he was already suffering from ill health. That didn't stop him from building a two-floored residence which he named, 'The House of Pleasure', later taking on a fourteen-year-old local girl as his native wife, or vahine. He was, in essence, a complete wrong-un. That, coupled with a very outspoken attitude towards the Catholic Church and the island's Gendarmerie, regularly labelling them as incompetent and corrupt, meant he quickly fell out of favour with the local administration.

Gaugin died within two years of his arrival - destitute, alone and riddled with syphilis. It's sad to consider that, like so many pioneering artists of his era, he ended his days penniless and living in obscurity, while his last painting went for $301 million in 2014. At the time, the most expensive piece of artwork ever sold.

He is buried in the Calvary Cemetery at the top of a hill, with a panoramic view overlooking Atuona Bay, fringed by the pink, white and yellow pastel flowers of the frangipani with their distinctive, captivating scent and a riot of other colourful shrubs - the most idyllic graveyard I've ever seen. While most of the tombs were marked with white crosses, Gauguin's simply had a round brown stone with his name painted on it. A replica of his statue *Oviri*, meaning wild, stood guard behind the crypt as per his wishes. There's another famous personage there too. Jacques Brel, the Belgium singer-songwriter who lived his final years in Atuona and had his body flown back from France to be buried only a couple of metres away from Gauguin's plot.

The town of Atuona is quaint with its beautiful Polynesian statues and carvings in every nook and cranny. Charming thatched buildings surround the *Tohua Pepeu*, the town square where all the local festivities are held. Close by is the Gauguin Museum with locally painted replicas of his most famous works and a huge arts and crafts centre. There is also a bank, but that is about it.

With little to do in town, I much preferred to go hiking into the mountains and find the ancient archaeological sites and petroglyphs - prehistoric rock carvings - that are dotted all over the island. So, the next day Sheila and I set off to explore the island's interior on foot. Hiva Oa is the most fertile of the Marquesas Islands and we walked past miles and miles of pamplemousse, banana and coconut plantations. Naturally growing fruits like mango and papaya sporadically popped up too, so we surreptitiously gorged ourselves on fresh fruit throughout the day.

It was tough hiking with legs and lungs that hadn't seen any cardiovascular action in ages, but it was well worth the effort when we finally reached the isolated ruins of an ancient religious site called a Me'ae a couple of hours of sweaty walking away, way up in the mountains.

That particular Me'ae consisted of a giant stone platform about the size of a tennis court - remarkably unscathed by the passage of time - surrounded by the crumbling walls and pavements of what must have served as the priest's accommodation and walkways. This was a place where human sacrifices were performed in the past for victory in war or to ensure a good harvest. Humans were slain on that very spot to consecrate the launch of a new canoe or even in celebration of the completion of the tattooing of the king's son. As much as I love boats, and tattoos for that matter, I certainly wouldn't be willing to die for them.

Up in the mountains, surrounded by old and wizened ancient trees we were afforded a stunning view over the island. It was impossible for me to equate the sense of peace and tranquillity I felt with the tales I'd read about ritual human sacrifice and cannibalism that took place on the very same stones I sat on.

Our trek back down to the harbour brought us into contact with some young workers on a copra plantation. Copra is the meat or kernel from the inside of a coconut which is first dried, then crushed to produce coconut oil. Once refined, it's used in a variety of ways, from cooking oils to the manufacture of skin and beauty products. The workers on the plantation, all male and in their teens, were very welcoming. They explained that the Tahitian government provided large subsidies for the production of copra, creating well-paid jobs for the youth still living on these remote islands in an attempt to stop their migration to the 'big' cities on the more affluent islands like Tahiti. The boys were happy to show us the ropes when they saw how interested we were in the job they toiled over for twelve hours every day.

They demonstrated how to split the coconuts with an axe and then expertly scraped out the white flesh with an extremely sharp, curved blade. The husks were discarded and the meat placed in a huge kiln. After a few days of drying, the flesh was bagged up into burlap sacks and sent by boat to Tahiti. They were kind enough to let me have a go at splitting and scraping the nuts, much to their amusement, as I proved to be pretty useless and would have sliced off a digit if I'd been allowed to continue. The harvesting of copra is a tedious and back breaking occupation and I couldn't help but admire those young men's efficiency, strength and stamina as they worked in such unbearably hot and humid conditions.

The Marquesas were also the birthplace of the first Tiki. A Tiki is a carving or sculpture of roughly humanoid form originally depicting the half human half god, *Ti'I* who, according to legend, was the first man on earth. Over time, Tikis took on many forms. Sculptured to represent gods as well as powerful and protective ancestral figures, they have since spread throughout the South Pacific. Hiva Oa has the largest of these ancient sculptures to be found anywhere in French Polynesia. This giant Tiki, standing at over two metres tall, is located on the north eastern corner of the island, near a village called Puama'u, but unfortunately far too long a distance to hike.

There is a sketchy network of dirt tracks linking the villages together, so we rented a 4x4 and traversed the mountains. The interior of the island comprises of a precipitous spine of volcanic mountains, ridges and remote valleys and a rugged all-terrain vehicle turned out to be the right choice. It was a nail-biting journey as I negotiated treacherous roads winding their way past completely exposed sheer drop-offs to the ocean, hundreds of metres below. We were all relieved when we finally arrived safely in Iipona, one of the best-preserved archaeological sites in the whole of the South Pacific.

As I wandered through the stunning site I was transported back to a time of mythology and magic, centuries before the influence of European adventurers and missionaries destroyed the traditional culture of the islands. Ancient Polynesians believed that all things, both animate and inanimate, were endowed with varying degrees of sacred, supernatural power. This power was known as 'mana' and it could be transmitted, inherited or nullified through various human actions. These religious beliefs permeated their entire culture and the stone Tikis are some of the few artefacts left that fully encapsulate this ancient way of thinking. Worshipped as gods, those imposing figures are impressive and symbolised the profound reverence the Marquesan tribesman had for the natural world surrounding them.

The largest Tiki in French Polynesia

Our time in Hiva Oa flew by and it was almost time to set sail again, but first I needed to transport all my gear to the recently arrived Wanderlust.

My time was up on Free Spirit and it was definitely time to move on. I said goodbye to the crew as well as a strained farewell to Bobby before jumping on a tender and heading to my new home.

Harry had only just arrived after waiting in the Galapagos an extra couple of days in the hope of securing an extra crew member, Juan Martin, an Ecuadorian who we'd met scuba diving. With insufficient time to organise Juan a visa before their departure, Harry had crossed the Pacific with just one other crew member. Exhausted after a challenging voyage, he'd sailed directly into the harbour instead of the anchorage outside and through a combination of tiredness and inexperience, he'd failed to notice all the yachts had stern anchors set. Motoring too close behind some French sea gypsy's dilapidated boat, he'd caught their stern anchor line with his engine's prop, careered into the Frenchman's hull and crushed the poor chap's wooden tender.

Consequently, my first few hours aboard Wanderlust were spent underwater, unwrapping the jammed prop, and the next few hours above water trying to placate a very angry - and justifiably so - long distance sailor. Not an ideal start, but an early precursor to the many problems I'd experience in the upcoming months sailing with Harry. Once an agreement on the damages was reached, a signed statement witnessed by the Gendarmerie and the yacht's insurance details provided, we were free to continue on our way.

We made a quick stop at Tahuata, a smaller island separated from Hiva Oa by a channel to the south a couple of miles wide. Our destination was Hanamoenoa Bay, a picture-perfect anchorage with crystal clear water and a white sandy bottom. Within minutes of anchoring I was in the water and exploring the reefs. The incredible visibility of over forty metres and a magnificent array of fish life kept me in the water for hours. Sheila had sailed into the idyllic cove the day before me and I was getting a little worried when I couldn't get hold of her in the anchorage throughout the day. After sundown I received a call over the VHF radio from the Finnish boat in our fleet saying they had Sheila aboard, but she was in some difficulty. She'd been swimming at night underneath one of the catamarans with its blue underwater lights on. These lights are incredible as they attract tons of fish. At first there's just a handful of small fish, but their numbers increase exponentially, bringing bigger and bigger fish as a feeding frenzy ensues. I've seen tuna, wahoo and barracuda all join the party and it can be a spectacular display of the ocean's food chain. On this occasion, a manta ray had joined the festivities, and while marvelling at the ray's aquabatics, Sheila swam straight into a jellyfish which wrapped itself around her face. Fortunately, she was wearing a dive mask which protected her eyes from any serious damage, but she sustained some excruciating stings on her face and throat.

I shot over in the tender and bathed her skin with vinegar. Vinegar alleviates the pain as it inhibits the stinging cells' discharge, but Sheila was left with several angry welts for weeks afterwards. Definitely not the welcome to paradise she'd hoped for and a painful reminder that there are plenty of creatures in the ocean to be wary of.

The next day I swam ashore to explore and to try and track down Stephen, a Marquesian hermit living on the beach. Sheila had met him the day before and told me he was a spear fisherman. I hoped to acquire a bit of local knowledge from him on which species were safe to hunt. Many of the reef fish in tropical waters ingest toxins from their food sources and Ciguatera food poisoning from eating the wrong fish must be avoided at all costs.

I didn't have far to look as we both emerged from the water at the same time. Of medium build with skin tanned to a dark brown, Stephen is tall and lean with brown hair and dark eyes - the picture of health. He carried a large parrotfish he'd just speared for lunch and I had my dry bag filled with a few tins of food and a jar of Nutella as gifts for him. Sheila told me he loved chocolate, so Nutella was the best I could do on short notice. To call him a hermit is a bit of an exaggeration though - Stephen welcomed any sailors who made the effort to visit him and traded fresh fruits for staple foods and treats. He had a slightly mad look in his eye, but some say the same thing about me, so we got along just fine.

After a delicious meal of baked fish and rice, we spent the afternoon talking about life, love and fishing. It turned out the three concepts were basically one and the same for both of us. He showed me around his home and explained how he survived, but never once mentioned the reason he'd chosen the life he lived. I didn't want to pry as some things are meant to remain a mystery, so I never asked. Throughout the day we were occasionally joined by his recent girlfriend, a French woman who had fallen in love with him on a previous trip to the island and left her husband in Tahiti to make a new life with him.

She was covered in insect bites and heat rash which, combined with her sullen disposition, made it look like things were not going quite to plan with her romantic adventures in paradise.

After a wonderful day and a spectacular sunset, it was time to bid a fond farewell to such a unique character. Sadly, our parting was hastened by some blood curdling banshee wailing issuing from his girlfriend somewhere deep in the dark forest. With a sad look in his eyes and a shaking of his head, Stephen shook my hand, wished me well and disappeared into the trees. I left his beach hoping one day he would find the love, peace and tranquillity he was searching for.

Our final destination in the Marquesas was Nuka Hiva, a hundred nautical miles to the north west. We headed there to pick up Ecuadorian Juan, who'd finally managed to secure a visa for French Polynesia. I'm unsure how they managed to land his plane though, as the runway should have been washed away by the torrential rain lashing down. I've never seen rain fall so hard and so heavily as it did in Nuka Hiva that day, but little did I know it was just a taster of what was to come in Tahiti.

In the end we picked up two new crew members on the island. Sheila was extremely unhappy on the boat she'd crewed on for months, because the owners, an Asian couple, barely gave her the time of day and she broke down in tears most nights we were together.

I talked with Harry about her mistreatment and he generously offered her a position on his yacht which she immediately accepted, and that was that. Sheila and I went from seeing each other every few weeks, to living together in a tiny cabin aboard Wanderlust, a true baptism of fire for any new relationship. The combination of a feisty, wilful Germanic woman who always speaks her mind and a headstrong South African who isn't good at being told what to do was a fiery one. There'd be trials and tribulations which would test the patience of a saint, and I'm no saint.

Chapter 9

Bob Marlin

13ºS, 142ºW

Life aboard Wanderlust quickly fell into the usual rhythm of watches and cooking, but mostly cleaning. Harry, a big, gruff man's man and his transpacific crew mate, Bob, were both in their mid-fifties. After sailing short-handed for over three thousand nautical miles together they'd had little time to look after the interior of the boat and internally, Wanderlust was filthy. Keeping the inside of your yacht clean is a prerequisite for a happy and healthy boat and their lack of attention resulted in a sailor's number one domestic nightmare, a cockroach infestation.

Sheila and I spent our first week of cohabitational 'bliss' disinfecting every nook and cranny of our new home. It wasn't pleasant being woken up in the middle of the night by curious creatures crawling over my face, so it was in our own vested interest to purge the problem quickly. Our new crew mate, Juan

Martin, was bright-eyed and bushy-tailed so we put him to work too. We worked our arses off and within days the boat began to resemble, if not a hospital, at least somewhere you wouldn't catch your death.

After nearly killing Bobby during my last fishing debacle, I sat down with Harry over a beer to discuss the matter.

'Are you happy for me to fish off your boat, mate?'

'Sure, no problem,' he replied, 'I haven't caught a single thing yet. Hopefully you'll have better luck than me.'

'Cool. I love fishing and I do it every day so fingers crossed our luck will change.'

I explained exactly what needed to happen on the yacht when we hooked a fish. He was all ears and one hundred percent game so I felt I could rest assured that if we were lucky enough to hook another beast, he'd at least try his best to help me land it.

Harry loved to see the sunrise, so he chose his watch to coincide with it every morning and for this reason it was crucial he knew what to do. The two most successful times for fishing are at dawn and dusk. I like to imagine the fish are hungry after not eating all night or they're getting a snack in before bedtime. The actual reason is that all bait fish use the cover of darkness to head up to the surface to feed on plankton, but in low light, big predators are harder to spot and use it to their advantage. The dim light helps to mask your lure too, so predators are more likely to mistake if for a live fish and strike. As darkness fell each night, I'd reel in my line but I'd instructed Harry to let it out again, with the lure sitting about twenty-five metres behind the boat, every morning before sunrise.

We were somewhere between the Marquesas and the Tuamotus in very deep water seldom sailed, never mind fished, and unlike most fishing tales, this one is in no need of embellishment. It all started early one morning, a few minutes after sunrise, when I was still fast asleep in my cabin. A familiar sound was attempting to invade my pleasant dreams, but I couldn't quite make sense of it. There are a few sounds in this world that excite me - the pop a bottle of wine makes when you uncork it is one and the hiss and fizz a cold beer makes when you crack it open is another, but of all the emotive sounds in the world, nothing comes close to the rush of adrenalin I get when I hear my fishing reel's ratchet screaming when I've hooked something big.

Although still dazed and confused, my sleep addled brain finally clicked into action. From a few feet above my head, my reel was going absolutely berserk. With the help of a rousing elbow from Sheila and Harry's muffled shouts of 'FISH', I was up the companion way and astern in a flash. Still bleary-eyed and wearing nothing but my boxer shorts, all I could see was Harry holding on to my fishing rod for dear life as a huge, glistening marlin repeatedly jumped clear of the water behind the boat.

'C'mon Daz,' he screamed, 'take this bloody thing off me, I can't hold on much longer.'

'YES,' I shouted triumphantly as I reached over. For a second there were four hands on the rod and it didn't feel too bad, but as soon as Harry released his grip, the sheer power of the marlin hit me and nearly pulled me into the water.

'Holy fuck!' I yelled.

Harry nodded, 'over to you now mate, I'll stop the boat.'

I screamed for Sheila to grab my life jacket and she helped me wriggle into it, tethering myself to the yacht while I kept fighting the fish. It was safety first and I knew only too well the dangers of this fight to the death.

At this crucial point there are three things that must be done to stand any chance of landing whatever's gobbled your lure for breakfast. Primarily you need to 'strike' the fish in order to set the hook. This entails rapidly heaving the rod back and forth to try and dig the hook's barb into the fish's mouth. Secondly, you need to slow the boat down as quickly as possible. Marlin, like most game fish such as tuna and wahoo, swim at an astonishing eighty kilometres an hour. When the fish is going in one direction as quickly as its mighty tail can take it and your boat is heading in the opposite direction, you run out of fishing line quickly. Therefore, it's crucial to curtail your boat's forward momentum immediately to give yourself the best chance of successfully 'turning the fish', which is number three on the list. Harry did an outstanding job on the first and Sheila and Bob helped out with the second, leaving number three down to me.

It was imperative I stopped the marlin's headlong race away from the boat. I knew if I could get the fish and the boat moving at the same velocity, and in the same direction, then I'd at least have a small chance of getting it onto the boat and subsequently onto the dinner table.

The rod bent in a huge arc and I feared I might not be able to turn the fish.

'Shit!' I cursed.

The marlin continued running away from the boat and I worried at some point it would create just enough slack in the line to spit the hook out or worse, that the sheer pressure would snap the line. I was rapidly running out of options and my reel was actually smoking as its lubricating oil began to cook from the friction.

I accidentally touched the reel's clutch mechanism with my thumb and screamed out in pain as my skin blistered from the intense heat. The clutch is located on the side of a reel and is used to try and control the flight of the fish as you crank up the resistance. The acrid aroma of burning oil and skin filled my nostrils as I frantically grabbed the bucket of rainwater at my feet, pouring it over the reel in a desperate attempt to try and cool down the internal mechanisms before they disintegrated. The marlin was winning this epic battle as it rapidly burned through two hundred metres of 100 lb strength line. I had no choice but to crank on the maximum drag available, which for all intents and purposes is supposed to stop the reel. Normally the trick is to increase the resistance in small increments, but this marlin was charging, and it was literally make or break time. The fish was so powerful my reel was still turning and I was so close to disaster I could actually see the knot I'd tied to connect the end of the line onto the spool. I don't know how, but miraculously I stopped the marlin's flight with less than a metre of line to go.

An intense half hour followed. For every metre of line I laboriously cranked in, the marlin took another metre back. Every sinew and muscle screamed out for mercy as my body took the strain while I pulled in inch after agonising inch of line, but just when I thought I was making a little progress, he'd get another burst of energy and undo all my hard work in seconds.

I saw the end knot on three occasions that morning but just managed to claw back enough line each time. The advantage swung back and forth for another thirty minutes until I finally made enough headway to think I had a chance of landing this monster.

The creature's strength was awesome and I reminded myself that while I was fighting for my supper, he was fighting for his life. What followed was a three-hour war of attrition. I played the fish by decreasing the drag on the reel and allowed him to run for short distances, all the while using the mechanical advantage of the rod and reel to slowly tire him out. It was a game of cat and mouse as I cranked the reel with all my might and painstakingly dragged the fish back towards the boat.

It was absolutely crucial to maintain pressure on the line at all times. One moment's inattention, resulting in a slack line, would be disastrous as a shake of the fish's head would dislodge the hook and my quarry would be gone in an instant.

With immense power and unbelievable stamina, the marlin never gave up a millimetre without a fight. Back and forth the pendulum swung, my total concentration never wavered for a second. It was a physical and mental fight right up until the end and it was anybody's game.

Time was starting to tell on both of us. After hours in the beating sun, my back and arms were burning from the effort of reeling him in. I was knackered and almost at the end of my endurance, but the marlin was gradually giving ground and I sensed he was also close to exhaustion.

After hours of back-breaking toil I finally had him within thirty metres of the boat and he knew it. In a last-ditch attempt to escape, he launched himself out the water, snapping his head back and forth, trying to slice the line with his serrated bill.

The crew was in position and knew their jobs - it was time for the last pull to get him on board - but I had miscalculated. I thought after his aeronautical display he would be spent but he was far from it. Every time I got him near the boat he found another burst of energy and ripped out more line. I don't know how many times he came close to snapping me off, but with a combination of luck and quick reflexes, I managed to release the clutch and let him run again, always just in the nick of time.

Another hour passed by and I was surviving on pure adrenaline. He was now just a few tantalising metres from the boat and I dared to believe victory might be heading my way. We were almost nose to bill now as he struggled just under the surface of the water, the biggest and most beautiful fish I've ever seen as the sun glinted off his silver, iridescent scales.

This was the most dangerous point of the fight. He was so close to the boat that the rod was no longer of any use. If I attempted to hoist the marlin out of the water the line would have snapped like a tinder dry twig. I called out to Sheila and she helped me put on protective gloves. With my heart in my mouth I knew it was now or never.

I looked at Sheila and smiled, 'take the rod sweetie.'

She did as I asked and nodded at me to indicate she was ready.

I leaned over the boat and grabbed the line with my gloved hands. My heart was almost jumping out of my chest, one wrong move and all my efforts would count for nothing. I pulled and pulled, hand-lining my prey the last couple of metres towards the boat. Harry was ready with the long gaff and as I summoned up the last of my energy, I heaved the marlin's head up to within inches of the side of the boat. Harry lunged down and managed to hook him, we were nearly there. I leaned over the stern and grabbed the marlin's bill, the half metre of prolonged upper jawbone that's rough like sandpaper. I don't know how we did it, but with our considerable combined strength we managed to get him up and over the transom and into the cockpit.

He wasn't finished yet though, as with a mighty swipe from his tail he caught Harry square in the face. The blow nearly knocked him off the boat and if he hadn't been such a big, powerful man he would have gone over. I looked on in horror as he steadied himself for a second and with one hand on the side of the boat for support he smiled and nodded he was okay.

I'd prepped everyone on exactly what to do. Sheila's job was to secure the fish's bill before it eviscerated somebody, a job she courageously undertook without a quibble. Juan's job was to pass me a large knife. I straddled the still bucking beast and drove the blade through the marlin's brain, finishing him off as quickly as possible.

I had fought the marlin for nearly four hours and the battle was finally over.

I lay on the cockpit seat, parallel with the two and a half metre marlin on the cockpit floor, in an exhausted stupor as the implications of what I'd achieved slowly sank in.

'I can't fucking believe it,' Harry said, 'it has to be a hundred kilos.'

Bob Marlin

I didn't have the strength to reply as I looked down at one of the mightiest species of fish in the ocean. I'd landed a marlin and attained the holy grail of sports fishing. I gazed around the blood-spattered crew - magnificent to a man (and woman). Without their help it would never have happened and I thanked them all. It was a surreal moment as we all looked on in disbelief at the slain monster that filled one entire side of the cockpit. He was truly a colossal gladiator of the sea and it seemed only fitting to give him a name and the legend of Bob Marlin was born. My job wasn't finished as I hauled myself up, wiped the blood from his face and set about removing my lure.

I had an introspective moment when I realised there was a second hook embedded in Bob's mouth, the remnants of a previous battle in which he was victorious. As I knelt over him there was a tear in my eye and a surge of sadness for the fallen warrior. In my mind there are only three reasons that excuse the killing of another creature. To protect yourself or those whom you love, to put an animal in pain out of its misery or - as had happened here - to eat it. With mixed emotions I thanked Bob Marlin for the privilege of our encounter and for the sustenance that his body would provide us in the weeks ahead. It had been an epic contest of one apex predator versus another, right down to the wire, the greatest fight of both our lives.

Chapter 10

Sharkarava

16°03'15S, 145°37'00W

The next island chain to the south west of the Marquesas is called the Tuamotus and it is comprised of the largest chain of atolls to be found anywhere in the world. There are about eighty of them and they're spread over an area roughly the size of Western Europe. Atolls paint a fascinating story of evolution and geological time, and they take up to thirty million years to form. The South Pacific is geologically incredible as you get to see the whole life cycle of these volcanic islands.

To begin with, an island is formed when an underwater volcanic eruption pumps out enough lava to break the ocean's surface. Over time this little volcano grows in magnitude, slowly rising higher and higher above sea level until, after many millennia, it finally runs out of magma and becomes extinct. These relatively new islands have steep faces and no coral reefs, just like Hiva Oa in the Marquesan Archipelago that I first visited. Over time, coral starts to attach itself to the submerged sides of the volcano and slowly begins to build a ring of living organisms around it. With the volcano no longer growing, gravity takes its toll and the heavy lump of rock gradually begins to sink back into the ocean, creating a gap between the volcanic cone and the surrounding coral reef. This is how a barrier reef is formed. As time marches on, gravity's relentless pull continues to drag the volcano down until its caldera - the large cauldron-like hollow in its centre - is swallowed by the sea, leaving behind a coral reef surrounding a lagoon where a once mighty mountain stood. This is an atoll.

Having read up on them, I could hardly wait to see my very first atoll, with the comical name of Fakarava. Fakarava is the second largest atoll in the archipelago and roughly rectangular in shape, sixty kilometres long and twenty-one kilometres wide. The total land mass, never more than a couple of metres above sea level, is only 1/50th of the area of the lagoon it encompasses. The entire atoll is only a tiny sliver of land surrounding a bright blue dot in the middle of the biggest ocean on earth.

In Fakarava the tidal flow has gouged two passes out of the encircling reef, allowing access to the lagoon from the north and south. We were heading for the northerly one, Passé Garuae, the largest pass to any atoll in the whole of French Polynesia and the safest option for our first ever attempt at accessing one of nature's true wonders.

Atoll passes are a daunting prospect for sailors. The huge bodies of water found in these lagoons are subject to the same tidal movements as the ocean surrounding them. As the tides rise and fall twice daily, an equilibrium must be maintained and all this water is squeezed back and forth through a tiny gap in a razor-sharp reef, creating currents of up to nine knots. To put that in perspective, most sailing boats can only motor at full throttle somewhere around seven knots. So, if you miss the slack water between tides and time it incorrectly, the consequences can be catastrophic. Many a yacht has been smashed on a reef or impaled on a coral head after being sucked into one of these overpowering currents. Fortunately, we'd timed our arrival perfectly, barely having to wait before the tide turned and we carefully motored our way into the lagoon.

After being tossed around by the ocean's swell for so long it was very strange to enter a body of water as flat as a lake that ran as far as the eye could see. With only one other boat in the anchorage we pretty much had the place to ourselves, and what an incredible spot it turned out to be. Never in my life had I experienced such contradictory seascapes. From the crystal clear and tranquil waters of the most beautiful blue lagoon imaginable, it was less than a hundred metre walk across a speck of white sand to where I was once again confronted with the raging open ocean swell. As waves remorselessly pounded the reef in front of me it was inconceivable that only a stone's throw away, just behind me, was the absolute peace and calm of water as flat and quiet as a frozen lake.

Sheila had done her research and our main reason for sailing to Fakarava was to bear witness to one of the highest concentrations of sharks to be found anywhere in the world, and when I say lots of sharks, I mean thousands of them. From the little black or white tipped reef sharks patrolling the lagoon, to lemon and nurse sharks resting in the shallows, to the multitude of grey reef sharks on the outer bank and even the occasional tiger shark or hammerhead. There were sharks everywhere. Affectionately called Sharkarava by scuba diving enthusiasts around the world, Fakarava is one of the world's premier diving destinations. Well, perhaps not if you don't like sharks, but if you love them like I do, then it's paradise.

A grey reef shark on patrol

Our first day of unforgettable diving was in the north pass. With nobody else about it was only Sheila and me booked on the dive. On most dive sites you normally have large groups of people from competing dive companies, all frantically churning up the water as they chase after each and every creature they come across. So with just the two of us it was rather romantic to be the only people on the dive boat and to have the ocean all to ourselves. Our instructor, Vincent, was a super cool French dude who'd decided to escape the rat race and just dive with sharks, instead of having to work in the city with them every day.

Our first dive was pretty mellow and took place during slack water as we explored one of the most beautiful coral gardens I'd ever seen. Spectacular corals of every shape, colour and size adorned every available surface and the variety and abundance of marine life was unparalleled. With visibility in excess of forty metres I could see some scattered shoals of sharks in the distance, ceaselessly patrolling the edge of the reef where the water dropped off into the abyss. There were huge shoals of snappers, fusiliers and red bigeyes and the occasional hump headed, thick lipped Napoleon Wrasse, the size of a park bench. With only eight hundred and fifty people living on the atoll, minimal pollution and no commercial fishing allowed, the ecosystem was in pristine condition and exactly the way the world's oceans are meant to be. Dive One was just the little starter in a four-course meal that would blow my mind.

Our second dive later that afternoon began after we forced our way through the pass and into the open ocean against an incoming tide. Even aboard a high-powered dive boat it was heavy going as we thumped into the incoming waves and got thrown around by the current. On arrival at the drop zone our dive instructions from Vincent were very clear. 'Sink like a stone and grab onto any rock within reach, otherwise you will get swept away.'

'Okay.'

'And stay together at all costs, a couple of weeks ago a diver got separated from the group and was swept away by the current.'

'No way,' I said.

'Yeah,' Vincent nodded, 'after a frantic search we located him four hours later about ten nautical miles into the lagoon.'

Vincent described how he'd been found, alive but petrified, bobbing away all on his own in shark infested water.

I don't even want to think about what must have been running through the poor guy's mind as he awaited rescue, watching the sun slowly sink towards the horizon as he began to imagine shark fins circling at dusk.

'Let me know if you have changed your mind,' Vincent grinned.

But I wasn't missing this for anything, no matter how many stories Vincent told me, and we plopped into the water and descended straight to the ocean floor. Once the three of us were all together on the same ledge, battling to hang on against the formidable current, Vincent gave the signal and we were off.

The incredible sensation that followed felt like flying underwater. In my fifteen years of scuba diving I'd never experienced the thrill of such a highspeed drift dive and it was absolutely exhilarating. With arms spread wide and a manic smile of pure delight plastered across my face, I was whipped through a kaleidoscope of underwater formations and bemused creatures.

By taking in a deep lungful of air I could soar up and over any incoming obstructions or fully exhale and swoop down like a bird of prey towards the sea floor.

I zipped past hordes of stationary sharks, languidly maintaining their positions within the current and flew through the middle of a giant shoal of fish that parted and then effortlessly reformed behind me. It was mind blowing stuff.

Vincent knew every nook and cranny of the dive and occasionally he stopped our headlong flight, ushering us over to a protected cove out of the tidal stream. From there we could peer over a ledge and see dozens of white and black tipped reef sharks, whiling away their time on the exposed sandy bottom, waiting for darkness when it was their time to hunt. These little sharks are completely harmless to humans so we had nothing to worry about, but they certainly aren't harmless to their prey. At a length of one and a half metres they are small enough to squirm through gaps in the coral and flush out hiding fish; extremely efficient predators in their own little niche.

It felt so liberating to glide effortlessly through the water, spinning and summersaulting while the current drove me onwards at five knots, way faster than I could possibly swim, and without the need to break sweat.

For an hour I felt like Peter Pan, accompanied by my very own Tinkerbell, as we adventured through Neverland. That once-in-a-lifetime drift dive turned out to be my favourite scuba dive, not only in Fakarava, but on the entire world trip. I hadn't considered how we'd be picked up at the end of it, but our trusty skipper followed our bubbles from the surface and was ready and waiting the moment we popped back up to the surface.

On the windy way home, Sheila snuggled contently into my arms as I wrapped her in my towel to keep her warm. I thought to myself how unbelievably lucky I was to have such an incredible woman by my side, willing and able to glide with me from one epic adventure to the next.

The following day it was time to navigate our way through the lagoon and anchor at the southern pass. We'd booked to dive there the following day, and with only thirty nautical miles to motor, it shouldn't have been too much of a problem. We'd all agreed to leave at ten in the morning to ensure we arrived at our destination well before sundown, but by midday we still hadn't moved and I was getting anxious. Whenever sailing in the vicinity of coral you need good sunlight, preferably from behind you to cut down the glare, to enable you to distinguish the different water depths and coral contours. The rule is, the darker the blue, the deeper the water you're sailing in. It lightens up through the entire range of blues, becoming white when you're over sand and in shallow water that is good for anchoring in. Any other colour, be it black, grey or brown, is always bad news as it indicates coral. Atolls are infamous for sprouting coral heads where you'd least expect them. Rock solid and razor sharp, they're nature's equivalent of a tin opener and can slice through a fibreglass hull like a warm knife through butter.

As Harry continued to tinker with something on board, I broached the topic of our departure time and I was dismissively told, 'After lunch.'

We finally left around one o'clock and although I didn't know it at the time, it would be a journey fraught with apprehension and angst.

I knew that Harry was new to sailing but I hadn't quite grasped how inexperienced he truly was. The first thing he suggested was to cut through the middle of the lagoon, following an old, unmarked channel on his charts which were decades out of date.

'We need to make up for lost time,' he said.

'Are you nuts,' I exclaimed, 'we are in the marked channel at the moment. It follows the edge of the reef and it is the only safe passage for a boat with our draft of nearly six foot.'

'Nah, bollocks to that,' he replied, 'these charts clearly show a route through the centre of the atoll. Can't you see the markers?'

I shook my head in disbelief.

'Let's get the spinnaker up and sail it.'

'Harry, the charts you are looking at are over twenty years old. Coral grows every day and up to a foot each year. From what your charts indicate, we should see twelve markers on that route and I can only count four. It's old, disused and downright dangerous.'

Instant manoeuvrability is crucial when dealing with coral, so I chose to ignore his ridiculous comment about sailing with the spinnaker.

I called Bob up from the galley to try and talk some sense into Harry.

'Marked channel or unmarked channel, what do you reckon Bob?'

Bob looked across at Harry.

'Perhaps we should just follow the other boats that are tucked just inside the reef, Harry. They look like locals and I guess they know best.'

Harry was well over six-foot-tall, built like a rugby forward and had hands the size of shovels. He'd spent his life on oil rigs, bullying other bullies into getting their work done. He let out a non-committal grunt and we continued on the same course, missing the turning point into his route of folly that would have heralded absolute disaster.

'Bob, is he for real?' I asked in a whisper, 'surely every skipper knows never to deviate from the marked channels.'

'Daz, I just have to make it to Tahiti where I can catch a plane out of here, believe me, there is no point confronting Harry. He will never back down. You have to cajole him into making the right decisions. It's driving me crazy but it's the only way to survive on this boat.'

Oh Jesus, I thought to myself, I'd jumped out of the frying pan on Bobby's boat and straight into Harry's fire.

The day just got worse. Once we were on the right track, Harry disregarded the electronic charts and almost missed out two marker buoys he just didn't see. After perceiving his adjustment to our course from below decks, and being conscious of the fact we had at least two miles left to travel on the same bearing before we needed to turn, I sprinted up to the helm, grabbed the wheel and swung the boat back towards the middle of the channel, narrowly averting disaster as we almost ran aground.

I looked at my watch and at the rapidly darkening sky. We had an hour left to go before sundown and it was obvious we were never going to make it to our planned destination on time. Taking Bob's advice, I tried to cajole Harry into anchoring up for the night before things got really silly. After a fifteen-minute discussion, I managed to convince him to turn back and head to the spot we'd passed ten minutes earlier, an anchorage which I'd marked on the navigational charts as a safety backup before we'd left. With a ton of clear water available, he still decided to drop the anchor between two coral heads as I tore my hair out in frustration. Fortunately, there wasn't a wind shift during the night so we remained unscathed, but I was seriously questioning Harry's decision-making capabilities.

It was a short motor the next morning to Tumakohua, the southern pass of Fakarava, a place which claims to have the highest concentration of grey reef sharks anywhere in the world. Before we could go and see for ourselves whether this was true, there was another Harry induced issue to deal with. Instead of taking one of the available mooring buoys another hundred metres further on, Harry decided to anchor just off the dive school. Once again, I tried to reason with him but to no avail.

We managed to drop the anchor on a tiny patch of sand, completely surrounded by coral, but we hadn't been stationary for more than a minute before the VHF crackled to life. 'This is a Unesco Marine Biosphere Reserve, it is not permitted to anchor here. Take a mooring buoy. Immediately.'

Suitably chastised, Harry gave the order to relocate, but surprise surprise, exactly what I'd warned him might happen, happened. The anchor chain had wrapped itself around a coral head and we couldn't budge it. Part angry, part embarrassed but completely mystified by Harry's intractability, I donned my free-diving gear, dived down the ten metres to the ocean floor, untangled the chain and solved another totally unnecessary fuck-up for my new skipper.

After another argument over whether to use one line or two to secure the boat to the mooring buoy (for safety you always use two warps just in case one gives way,) I'd had just about enough of Harry's bullshit and swam ashore with Sheila, absolutely fuming.

As I waded through the shallows any negative thoughts about Harry and his incompetence vanished as I marvelled in open mouthed astonishment at a picture-perfect postcard scene straight out of a dream. A couple of ruffled coconuts palms framed the scene, gently swaying in the light breeze next to thatched wooden bungalows on stilts, daintily perched above a piercing blue sea that gently caressed a tranquil, white beach. A couple of reef sharks leisurely cruised the coastline in an ocean sparkling with vitality. The scene was so serene it almost felt sacrilegious to set foot ashore and disturb the unspoilt sands. I could have died and gone to heaven, but it seemed I was already there.

For our next scuba dive we headed down to around twenty metres in the middle of the southern pass and I'd never seen anything like it. There were sharks everywhere! Magnificent two-metre-long, savagely sleek eating machines as far as the eye could see, gracefully cruising around in search of food. Their numbers were staggering with somewhere between five and six hundred sharks in an area the size of a football field.

Unless you have seen a shark swimming it is almost impossible to imagine how effortlessly these huge predators make their way through the water. With a languorous sweep of their tail, they glide elegantly through the ocean in slow motion, until they turn and the flash of a white underbelly signals that another creature's life violently cut short. Their power, speed and agility were awe inspiring as they surgically plucked off any stragglers from the milling shoals of fish. Even though there was a lot of other aquatic life about, it should be impossible for so many sharks to coexist in such a small space, but this atoll has a naughty little secret.

Fakarava is the place where fish come to procreate. Throughout the year, massive aggregations of various fish species descend on the pass to spawn. From giant groupers to sturgeon and a host of others, tens of thousands of eager fish congregate to breed, and when they do, a feeding frenzy ensues. Massimo was to experience one of these feeding frenzies first-hand. He'd decided to go spear fishing off the back of his boat in the next atoll to the north west of Fakarava called *Toau*. After searching the ocean for sharks and not seeing any, he got in range of a large wahoo and fired, killing it instantly. In the blink of an eye his vision filled with a dozen sharks, tearing into his prey and then turning on him. As he finned back towards his boat, screaming for help, the grey reef sharks attacked his retreating fins before he scrambled back onto his boat. Normally unflappable, Massimo had made it through his considerable range of expletives in four different languages on the way back.

His metre-long metal spear had been twisted in an s-bend, and serrated bite marks covered his expensive fins. It was a stark reminder that grey reef sharks, although docile in normal conditions, can become extremely dangerous the second they smell blood in the water. We finished off the day with another drift dive through the pass and as exciting as it was, I don't think anything will ever compare to the rollercoaster ride I experienced in the north pass.

It was way too short a stay in the Tuamotus, but we knew from the start of setting off with Harry that he had to get to Tahiti quickly in order to catch a flight to the UK for a health check-up. He almost didn't make that flight. Harry once again ignored the charts while leaving the atoll and aimed directly for the same reef we'd navigated around the day before when looking for a place to anchor. I once again grabbed the wheel, pointed out the cardinal marker warning of the imminent danger, and admonished him for such carelessness. He wasn't just a danger to himself and the yacht, his incompetence was endangering my life and that of the other crew members too.

At that point I vowed to be extra vigilant at all times, hoping we'd make it to Tonga and my next ride, before any major calamity ended my bid to sail around the world.

Chapter 11

Tattoos and Teahupo'o

17°32'30S, 149°34'15W

The Society Islands are the largest and most populated islands in French Polynesia. The biggest and most famous one is Tahiti and that's where we were heading next.

In my darkest winter hours, wrapped up in a sleeping bag and under a duvet, freezing my ass off in my draughty London attic room, I'd dreamt of escaping to Tahiti and it got me through some dreary weeks of work. My favourite sailor of all time, Bernard Moitessier, settled in Tahiti after competing in the first solo non-stop sailing race around the world, called the Golden Globe. Instead of finishing the race and heading back to England after circumnavigating once, he decided to continue sailing another halfway around the world again in order to reach Tahiti. He built himself a hut, went spear fishing, grew fruit trees and retired from the modern world to escape civilisation and *save his soul*. So I had high hopes of finding my very own little paradise in Papeete, the capital of French Polynesia.

On arrival, we were greeted with torrential rain which didn't let up for the next fourteen days. Every hour, there were rain showers and the boat became a sticky, humid mess and impossible to ventilate. Bernard's books were written almost fifty years ago and things have changed dramatically since then, not just in French Polynesia, but everywhere else in the world. The marina in Papeete is right in the heart of the city, next to a three-lane highway which certainly wasn't there when Bernard found his little paradise. It was noisy and polluted and the constant daily influx of thousands of cruise passengers didn't help either. This resulted in astronomical prices and the accompanying hustle and bustle I'd gone sailing to escape; a far cry from the palmed beach tranquillity I'd always imagined it to be.

To say I was underwhelmed by Papeete is an immense understatement. Sheila and I did have the boat practically to ourselves though, as Juan was off gallivanting most of the time, so it was our little honeymoon. Since we were stuck in the same place for a fortnight, I decided I'd spend my time and money wisely and get myself tattooed.

Tattoos, although initially made famous by Captain Cook's expeditions and thought by many to have originated from Polynesia, have in fact been around for millennia. Examples can be found in almost every corner of the globe, but the Polynesians have an unbroken tattooing tradition that covers almost two thousand years. So even if they didn't invent tattooing, they mastered the art form and it became a fundamental part of their culture. Used to indicate social status, genealogy and one's rank within society, their beautiful tattoos are filled with distinctive signs and symbols, expressing an individual's identity and personality.

In the pouring rain I wandered around town from one tattoo shop to the next, with a very specific idea of what I wanted to get done. I started to get irritated when the various tattooists pointed me towards their portfolio catalogues and told me to choose something I liked. For me, a tattoo is an extremely personal artistic expression of who you are at a certain point in your life. It's a way of permanently documenting the important events that happen to you and thus should be unique and original. Getting a tattoo from a scrap book goes against all the things I believe a tattoo should stand for. So with a heavy heart I walked into the final studio on my list, prepared to be disappointed.

I was welcomed into the shop by a mountain of a man, heavily built and over six foot tall. He was covered from head to toe in traditional Polynesian tattoos and exuded the aura of a mighty warrior. He'd have cut an intimidating figure if it wasn't for his mischievous eyes and gentle smile. I sensed immediately he was the genuine article and with ninety five percent of his body covered in ink, totally committed to his art form.

With little preamble we started to discuss what I had in mind.

I wanted a marlin over my right flank to commemorate Bob Marlin, my first ever monstrous game fish, and a shark on my left side to pay homage to those powerful creatures so abundant in the South

Pacific. Tito, as he was called, was genuinely excited about the project.

'Down the ribs is very painful,' he said.

I pulled up my shirt to show my chest and stomach tattoos.

'I can take it.'

He took one long look at me, smiled, and booked off the entire following day so we could get started.

The next morning in the tattoo parlour, Tito explained the meaning of the various symbols found in the Polynesian tattooing tradition, all based on the four elements: water, earth, wind and fire. For example, shark's teeth represented power and courage, symbolising protection and fertility and fishhooks represented strength, determination and provided safe passage across water. The list went on. Tito asked me questions about my life, my family and all my adventures. He then proceeded to hand draw a unique and personalised design for the next three hours, incorporating my life story into the sketch. Once we were both satisfied with the design, we took a quick lunch break before it was time to suck it up and get on with the torture.

I have many tattoos in a variety of tender places, but nothing had prepared me for the pain and discomfort I was about to experience. With my arm stretched over my head as I sat uncomfortably twisted over a bench, Tito proceeded to carve up and down my rib cage for seven long hours. The soft, flexible flesh in between my rib cage was bearable as the needle dug in but as it touched the thin flesh above each rib, I was in considerable discomfort. The human body only has a certain amount of natural pain killers and I ran out of happy juice with about an hour to go. For the final onslaught of agony, Tito finished off the marlin's tail section near my groin and the head under my armpit. By the end of the day we were both exhausted but super happy with the result.

I returned three days later for the next session of seven hours of pain. He crafted the shark on my left flank in the same manner, but it didn't hurt half as much. As with most things in life I find that doing something for the first time is always the hardest, but the human brain and body are amazingly adaptable, and things seem to get easier with experience. It was another exhausting day for both of us but worth every second of the pain and discomfort when Tito turned to me and said, 'man, you've sat straight through two, seven-hour sessions without flinching. You have the mana of a warrior. If you're around long enough for those to heal I'd like to take you surfing some time.'

I thanked him profusely for his unerring effort in indelibly stamping me with the symbols of his culture, but the surfing would have to wait until my next trip to Tahiti. We only had a few days left and it takes longer than that for damaged skin to mend. To be identified as a warrior by somebody who epitomised one was compliment enough. Being offered an opportunity to brave the waves with such a highly respected local was almost unheard of, and I felt truly honoured by his sentiment.

Tahiti wasn't all pain and rain. Stephen and Belle, the Australians, had rented a car and invited Sheila and me to go exploring. Stephen had been a competitive body boarder down in Margaret River, so there was only one destination he had in mind.

Nestled down in Tahiti, Iti, in the south western section of the island is one of the most mythical waves in the world, the fearsome Teahupo'o, known as the world's heaviest wave.

Due to the unique formation of its extremely shallow reef, Teahupo'o actually breaks below sea level and the entire wave folds over itself. This creates a very distinctive hollow wave that's incredibly powerful and often has a lip as thick as the wave is tall. This incredible hydrodynamics makes for one of the scariest barrelling waves in the world, and in big swell an absolute bone crunching monster is born. Imagine a ten-metre wall of water hurtling towards you as it rears up and begins to topple. Thousands of tons of water is lifted into the air and comes crashing down onto a ragged and razor-sharp crescent shaped reef less than a metre below the surface. Then contemplate jumping on a board and charging that beast. Just the thought of it scares the shit out of me. After much negotiation and pleading, we managed to hire a boat to take us out to the break a few hundred metres offshore. With a striking backdrop of luscious green mountains and palm fronted beaches, the skipper carefully navigated his way through the reef and idled the boat on the edge of the safety channel where the wave terminates. It was the time of year when the annual World Body Boarding Championships were being held, so the wave was off limits to us amateurs. Even so, it was an incredible experience to see some of the world's best riders ripping it up on one of the most hallowed waves on earth.

Our time in Tahiti wasn't complete without a trip into its mountainous interior. On the only day forecast to have light rain, Sheila and I booked an excursion and jumped onto the back of an open topped 4x4 heading inland. The rain held off for all of five minutes while we bounced in the back of the pickup truck up some seriously steep terrain. We were soaked through, uncomfortable and cold from start to finish - not normally my idea of a good time on land, as I got enough of that at sea, but this was different. It was absolutely worth it to observe the most amazing waterfalls I'd ever seen, cascading down a single mountain range. I stopped counting at two hundred, because the entire mountainous vista before me was overrun with raging vertical rivers of water. I'd never imagined so many waterfalls could occur simultaneously but I guess that's par for the course when it pisses it down for weeks.

The only problem with all the precipitation was we had crossed a dyke to get there, and by the time we headed back it was well and truly flooded. There were markers on the dyke with a foot-high yellow strip on the bottom and another red strip a foot above that. Yellow was still safe but when the water went above the two-foot-high red section of the bollards, there was no more crossing as the water flow was powerful enough to bowl over a vehicle. The raging torrent visibly inched its way up the bollards as the pickup painstakingly crawled its way across. At the last moment, as the front wheels edged out of the dyke, the back end slewed towards the raging torrent and for a moment I thought the driver had misjudged it, but he gunned the accelerator and we lurched forward to safety. We'd made it through, but only just.

And yet, if the 4x4 hadn't made it and we had been stranded, I wouldn't have minded being stuck in the mountains for a couple more days. The thought of going back to our musty old cabin wasn't a pleasant one.

Much of our time in Papeete was spent whiling away the hours in a bar drinking with friends while we waited for the sun to make an appearance through the clouds. One afternoon on a particularly wet and windy afternoon, in walked Big Steve, another skipper in the fleet, wearing his favourite t-shirt. It was the size of a tent and had 'I AM VIKING' emblazoned on the front of it. I had to smile, because Big Steve wasn't Scandinavian, but English through and through, although I'm sure there was some Nordic blood pumping through his gargantuan frame. Big Steve was a bearded bear of a man, standing two metres tall with a build to match. He would have been a really imposing figure if he wasn't so quick to laugh and he always sported an ear to ear grin. I'd helped him and his lovely wife, Lynda, to do some maintenance on their yacht a few months before. I think he was pretty scared of heights. At one hundred and thirty kilos he wasn't exactly built to climb masts and I didn't relish the idea of hoisting his bulk to the top either. So I'd offered to be the mast monkey for the day and we'd been mates ever since.

It had been a few months since we'd last met up, so we had a lot to talk about since I'd left my last yacht.

'How are you doing Dazzla,' the big friendly giant bellowed as he perched next to me with a pint glass dwarfed in his hand.

I told him about Bobby and how irritated I'd been on our last voyage. I'd paid my crew fees of one thousand pounds all the way up to Australia and now that I'd moved onto a new boat, he'd refused to refund me the difference I felt I was owed. I went on for a minute or two before Big Steve placed one of his giant paws on my shoulder.

'I didn't ask how WERE you doing buddy, I asked you how ARE you doing,' he said, 'don't waste your energy focusing on the bad things that have happened to you because there's nothing you can do to change the past. Focus on the good things happening in the present.'

It was a profound moment.

He was right. I was in the South Pacific, living my dream and all I was concerned about was some petty boat politics from months before. Instead of enjoying the fun and positive camaraderie of a friendly reunion, I'd brought up some negativity from the past which could have ruined the day if Big Steve hadn't been so forthright in putting me straight.

'You're absolutely right mate,' I replied as I sidestepped the quagmire of negativity I'd almost fallen into, 'he's not worth the wasted energy.'

'That's the spirit my boy, and on the topic of spirits, my worldly advice isn't free so be a good lad and go and get me some rum.'

He laughed loudly and sent me sprawling towards the bar with a hearty backslap.

Since that encounter I've always tried to remember Big Steve's advice.

Positivity forever, negativity never.

As I once read somewhere, 'The past is a ghost, the future a dream, all we have is now.'

Harry's return from his two-week medical trip to the UK heralded the beginning of the end of my patience with his incompetence. Harry had flown Juan into the Society Islands from the Galapagos, but neither of them had paid much attention to the length of the visa he'd been granted. By the time Juan got around to doing anything about extending his month's stay, it was too late as it had already expired and he was technically an illegal immigrant. Maritime law holds the skipper of the boat responsible for their crew so Harry headed to the relevant authorities to try and fix the matter. They were furious, and after fingerprinting him for breaking the law, they threatened him with incarceration even though it was mainly Juan's fault. In the end, Harry was only given a serious reprimand by immigration and was lucky not to be fined heavily. Juan was told to leave the country immediately and forced to book a flight that day. The closest airport he could fly to was in Rarotonga in the Cook Islands, the next archipelago west and out of the Society Islands. So, our plans were changed. We could no longer head to Suwarrow with the fleet, but instead needed to get to Cook Island's capital city instead. This precipitated one of the best experiences on the whole trip, but also the worst.

After Juan's hasty departure, we fortunately had enough time to briefly visit a few of the neighbouring islands surrounding Tahiti before we had to head west to pick him up again.

Joining us for a week of cruising was Jay, a bonkers British lad and a scuba diving instructor friend of Sheila's. By bonkers I mean just that. He's the only person I've ever met who thought it would be a good idea to go surfing next to a flooded river mouth during the sardine run in South Africa, the most dangerous time and place ever to go surfing. Not surprisingly, during this shark feeding frenzy, a bull shark took a liking to his backside. He needed over a hundred stitches in his arse, but the nutcase was back in the water surfing a month later, after his stitches were removed. With a great sense of humour, an innate love of the ocean and a fondness for silly alcohol fuelled antics, we got on like a house on fire.

We visited Moorea, Raiatea and Tahaa before he had to jump ship and go back to Indonesia to reopen his dive shop. I was invited to dive with him any time I found myself in Southeast Asia and I planned to take him up on the offer.

A Tahitian outrigger canoe and a traditional dwelling

Moorea, Raiatea and Tahaa are pretty islands, but they are all totally eclipsed by the breath-taking beauty of Bora Bora. If you were tasked to design the most exquisite island in the world then you'd struggle to surpass the enchanting vision of Bora Bora. Looking almost like a giant green sombrero perched on the Pacific, the island has two extinct volcanoes that rise at its centre and then gradually taper down to the water's edge. This luscious foliage is surrounded by a beautiful turquoise blue lagoon and pristine coral reef. With a sprinkling of tiny islets, called motus, dotting the lagoon and a multitude of sharks and rays in the crystal-clear water, it's simply breath-taking. Stilted bungalows and walkways creep like tendrils from the shore over the perfectly calm and protected waters, somehow enhancing the island's beauty instead of detracting from it.

When the ancient Polynesians named it 'Pora Pora Mai Te Pora' which translates into 'Created by the Gods', they got it absolutely spot on.

Sheila and I spent our days cruising around in the tender, searching for sharks and manta rays within the lagoon and our nights sipping cocktails and pretending to be newlyweds like the dozens of other couples surrounding us on the most beautiful island of them all.

Chapter 12

Another close call

21°12'15S, 159°47'00W

With the course change dictated by Juan's visa fiasco, we sailed to Rarotonga to pick him up. There's only one harbour of commercial significance on the island so we headed towards Avatiu.

The harbour is situated on the northern coast, facing directly north with only a small breakwater protecting a little marina designed for fishing boats with very shallow draughts. This makes the harbour unusable for larger vessels when the wind blows from a northerly direction as there is nothing to stop the waves rolling directly through its unprotected mouth.

It was around five hundred nautical miles from Bora Bora and I calculated it would take us approximately four days to get there. With steady winds from the east it was a serene voyage, but as we drew closer to the island the wind began to back further and further northwards. This worried me and I brought it to

Harry's attention, clearly stating that if it shifted any further north, it would be impossible to stay in the harbour at Avatiu as there'd be no protection from the elements. I assumed he'd got the message as we motored in and moored in the Mediterranean fashion, stern to the wharf with our anchor dropped sixty metres in front of us and the bow facing towards the harbour entrance. As per usual there were the normal formalities of customs and immigration and so our problems began.

Harry hadn't realised that for many Polynesian islands - as for most islands around the world - you need to register online in advance before entering their territorial waters. Normally the WARC completed these formalities for each boat, but as we'd taken a detour and split from the fleet, it had been overlooked by the skipper.

Harry had a pretty uncomfortable conversation with the port authority for over an hour before they allowed us to check in but with a strict warning to follow protocol or we'd be heavily fined and banned from entering in the future.

Meanwhile, I'd kept a wary eye on the weather and I was getting worried.

There was a Swedish yacht tied up with an elderly couple onboard a few boat lengths down from us. I shouted over to them, 'watch the wind guys, you don't want to be in here if it switches any further to the north!'

They acknowledged my warning but didn't seem anxious.

Throughout the morning the wind had been slowly creeping north and it wasn't far off blowing directly into the harbour by the time Harry finished with the bureaucrats. When we'd entered the harbour, the water had been as calm as a mill pond, but now I could see the swell starting to edge its way around the harbour wall.

'Harry, this isn't a good place to be,' I said, 'we need to get out of here and into deeper water.'

'Quit your whinging,' he snapped back, 'you're always on my case about something or other,' he replied as he clambered aboard.

Juan, all smiles and happy to see us after being marooned on the island for two weeks, jumped on board too.

Within a few minutes the swell had increased and the lines we used to secure the yacht to the wharf began to grind against the metal boat cleats they were attached to, and the anchor chain was groaning under the strain as the yacht rode up and down on the incoming wavelets.

Realising we were facing impending doom I remonstrated with Harry, 'we need to get out of this harbour immediately, it's a death trap!'

To my absolute astonishment he levelled his gaze and shouted back at me, 'this is my fucking yacht, Daz, and you're just a crewman! I make the decisions on my boat and we are staying put for the night.'

I couldn't believe my ears and shook my head in disbelief. The wind and waves were just about to rip through the harbour mouth and we were a few minutes away from getting pummelled into oblivion.

I'd had enough of him. I stormed down the companion way and into my cabin, closely followed by Sheila, grabbed all of my valuables and electronic gear and stuffed them into dry bags. If worse came to worst, I'd be ready to abandon ship.

'What's going on, what are you doing?' she asked.

'Pack all of your important belongings, the pig-headed fool is going to shipwreck us.'

As if in answer to my last proclamation, I felt the first big wave hit the boat, the bow bucked like an angry stallion and I knew exactly what had happened.

'What's happening?' Sheila screamed with panic-stricken eyes.

'The anchor's been ripped from the ocean floor, get on the stern and do exactly what I tell you.'

She was momentarily frozen with fear.

'C'mon Sheila, we've only got one chance to save this boat,' I shouted over my shoulder as I sprinted upstairs.

Harry stood in the cockpit in open-mouthed horror. The boat heaved up and down in the growing swell and he understood we were in deep shit, but there was no time for recriminations, just action. I'd already been shipwrecked once before and I wasn't going to go through that horrible experience again, so I immediately took charge and sprinted to the bow. I'd purposefully left the electric windlass on (the motor that pulls in the anchor chain), just in case of such an emergency, and I dragged the anchor backwards in an attempt to keep the bow facing directly into the waves. If, for any reason, the wind and waves caught the beam of the boat, we would be pushed side-on into the unforgiving cement dock and there'd be no escape as the waves smashed Wanderlust out of existence.

I managed to keep the bow pointing into the wind as I screamed commands to the crew over the howling wind.

'Harry for fuck sake!'

He was still standing in the cockpit, motionless, gazing out at the harbour mouth.

'Harry, snap out of it and switch the bloody engine on.' I looked around, 'Juan, Juan, where the hell is Juan?'

'I'm over here Daz,' came back his faint reply.

I looked towards the sound of his voice and focussed on him. I couldn't believe what I was seeing. For some god forsaken reason, he was standing in the tender and almost getting crushed between the boat and dock. Harry had sent Juan to attach more warps to the dock, exactly the opposite of what was required, and the tender was bouncing around like a kid's bath toy. We were minutes away from total annihilation and now Juan's life hung in the balance too.

'Get back on the boat Juan, we've got to get out of here, NOW!' I screamed.

Sheila was above deck, rooted to the spot and as white as a ghost as she looked on in disbelief.

There was no time for niceties as I screamed at her too. 'SHEILA, get moving! I need you to detach the stern warps on my signal. Grab the boat knife and cut them if you have to.'

My authoritative voice galvanised her back into action and she sprang to the task.

I looked over to the Swedish yacht as they looked on in utter despair so I screamed at them too. 'Get the hell out of here before it's too late.'

Finally, there was movement on their deck as they sprang into action.

With the anchor chain irrevocably shortening as I dragged it backwards, I only just managed to maintain the boat's bow into the wind. Juan scrambled aboard and secured the tender, both of them miraculously unharmed, and I sent him back to help Sheila.

'Full power ahead Harry,' I screamed over the roaring wind and mimed pushing the engine full throttle in case he couldn't hear me.

With only fifteen metres of anchor chain still left in the water and only seconds to spare before total disaster, Harry gunned the engine and we began to inch our way forward, away from the concrete dock.

'Sheila, Juan, warps off now!' I bellowed, just as I felt the anchor break free from the ocean floor for the last time and it clattered home into its cradle on the bow seconds later.

Juan and Sheila acted on my command as they threw their lines towards the dock and away from the propeller. Getting a rope wrapped around the prop at that point would have been game over. With the full fury of thirty-five knots of wind, the waves rocked the boat back and forth as if it were a giant seesaw. We were in for a wild ride as we all held on for dear life.

I looked back to see how our Swedish neighbours were coping and heard the horrific sound of the boat's stern platform grinding against the unrelenting concrete dock. I watched on in horror as the carnage unfolded with each and every wave driving them back into the pier. With only two people on board, they hadn't been quick enough to get away, and every collision sent a dagger through my heart. There was stunned silence aboard as we gradually made headway out of the harbour and into the safety of deep water. It had taken less than two minutes from the time I took charge on the anchor to when we'd dropped our stern lines, but they were the longest two minutes of my life. There wasn't much talking aboard for the next few hours as we sailed to the south of the island, in shock from what had just transpired.

We would have to wait out the northerly wind overnight in the lee of the land before it was safe to return, exactly where we should have been all along. With no thanks from Harry for my efforts in saving his yacht, he did manage the moronic statement that what we should have done was put down two anchors instead of just one.

I bit my tongue. I wanted to throttle him but instead, I counted to ten. In essence, dropping two anchors would have made it twice as difficult to escape from somewhere we should never have been in the first place.

That settled it for me. Harry had no idea what he was doing – he was an accident just waiting for a place to happen. Beware of an incompetent skipper with a big ego, they're a very dangerous breed indeed.

The next morning the wind switched back to its normal easterly direction and it was safe to head back to the harbour. Our warps were still attached to the dock, as were the Swede's cut lines, but their boat was nowhere to be seen. I'd watched them disappear on the radar the night before, so they weren't coming back into port for love or money, they'd done a runner. God knows what sort of state their boat was in. Harry contemplated doing the same thing the night before, until I pointed out that none of us had been checked out from the island, and Juan wasn't even on the crew list as he'd flown in. I didn't even want to imagine the bureaucratic nightmare that would have caused at our next port of entry. From that point on, my main job aboard Wanderlust was one of damage limitation; taking all of my vigilance to stop Harry making any more stupid and dangerous decisions.

With no imminent threat from the weather as the winds stabilised, it was safe to leave the boat in the harbour and we got a chance to explore Rarotonga. It's a beautiful little island and one of the only populated ones I'd visited that hadn't been overrun by commercialism.

There are no high-rise buildings, no McDonalds, no chain stores and during our bicycle ride around the island we didn't even see one set of traffic lights. Best of all though is their money. I collected notes and coins from every country I visited on the trip as mementoes of my travels, and nowhere has cooler money than the Cook Islands. Their main currency is the New Zealand Dollar but they have their own money in circulation too. The coins range from triangular shapes to dodecagons (twelve sided), with the $1 coin scallop edged. But best of all is their old three-dollar bill. On the front of the note is a naked girl surfing a barrelling wave while straddling a shark. On the back is an outrigger canoe and a Tiki with a large, dangling phallus. Priceless.

All travellers are in search of that unique, once in a lifetime experience which can't be bought, where you're so far off the beaten track you're not treated like a human cash machine but instead made to feel thoroughly welcomed because visitors are such a rarity. I was lucky enough to have that experience a couple of days later on Palmerston Island, a tiny little coral atoll about three hundred miles north west of Rarotonga. It was a long haul to Niue and our next rendezvous with the fleet, so we decided to pop into Palmerston on the way - an island only accessible by boat and one of the remotest permanently inhabited islands in the world. Discovered by James Cook on the 16th of June 1774, it's the only Cook Island where English is the native language and its fascinating history all started with one man.

In the 1860's William Marsters from Leicestershire, England, arrived on the island to set up a copra plantation with his wife, Akakaingaro, the daughter of a Cook Island royal chief. He also brought along two of her cousins whom he later married, splitting the island into thirds with two lines of palm trees, an ingenious way of dealing with the sticky situation of having three wives. In 1892 he was granted possession of the island by Queen Victoria.

From humble beginnings William created a dynasty, fathering twenty-three children, one-hundred-and-thirty-four grandchildren and his descendants number in excess of fifteen hundred people, all scattered around the South Pacific. He accomplished all this in seven years but sadly died from malnutrition when a blight destroyed his coconut crop.

The atoll is made up of four tiny islands surrounded by a coral reef with an extremely shallow and twisting entrance that is only navigable with local knowledge so there is no way in unless you're invited. We certainly didn't have to worry about an invite though as we were only the fourth yacht to visit that year, bringing the total number of guests to a staggering twelve and the islanders couldn't wait to meet some fresh faces.

After taking a mooring buoy on the leeward side of the island, a guy called Bob Marsters picked us up on his aluminium fishing boat and took us ashore to explore. I'd heard of the fabled Polynesian hospitality before but even that must pale in comparison to how we were treated by Bob, his family, and all the rest of his extended family on the island. On Palmerston, the three branches of the dynasty take it in turns to 'adopt' visitors, and by adopt I literally mean you become part of their family for the entirety of your stay. They feed you, house you and do everything in their power to make you feel welcome.

Chatting over a mouth-watering lunch of parrot fish, rice and chicken his wife had started to prepare as soon as she saw our sail on the horizon, we found out Bob was actually the Major of the island and its sixty-one other inhabitants. The inhabitants were all Marsters, except for two Christian missionary schoolteachers and an Aussie lad doing some research.

'Eh girl,' Bob shouted to his daughter, 'go and get these thirsty sailors another coconut.'

As I pulled out my wallet to pay for them Bob began to chuckle.

'Money never changes hands on this island my friend. Whatever somebody needs, somebody else provides. We share everything we have with each other and nobody ever goes hungry.'

'You never use money?' I enquired, fascinated by the concept.

Bob shook his head, 'with each other, never. But today plenty of money will change hands because the big ship that sailed in with you this morning is our supply ship and it's six months overdue.'

He explained that on a tiny island in the middle of nowhere, the arrival of the supply ship was the equivalent of Christmas, New Year's Eve and carnival all rolled into one. Crammed with items essential to the islanders' survival, it was their lifeline to the outside world, apart from an occasional cruising yachtsman.

'I will take you to the supply ship later, but first I'll show you the island. It isn't big, but it's been my family's home for over one-hundred-and-fifty-years.'

We set off on a tour of the island with an entourage of excited children following in our wake. Our first stop was a little hut surrounded by a vegetable garden; the only cultivated plants other than coconuts I saw anywhere else on the island. Sitting on the porch with his head in his hands was Derek, the Aussie researching the reefs, looking rather distressed.

'Eh Derek, what's the matter with you?' Bob enquired, 'I've brought some guests to meet you.'

Derek looked up and with tear stained cheeks he pointed towards two giant chest freezers sitting like tombstones in his front garden. We ambled over and Bob took the liberty of opening one up to see what the problem was.

'Oh shit,' Bob exclaimed with a face that mirrored Derek's sadness, 'this is bad. Real bad.'

Derek burst into tears, 'they're destroyed, everything is destroyed. I've been waiting a year for this delivery and it's all utterly useless,' Derek sobbed as I leaned over and peered into the metal hulks.

Derek's delivery from the supply boat had arrived that morning, but both freezers were completely waterlogged, and judging by the contents they'd been sodden for some time. The saltwater ingress had corroded the batteries he had sent over from New Zealand and the liberated acid destroyed everything else. There were a dozen solar powered shower units he'd imported to improve the islanders' standard of living but they were rusted to hell. The seeds he'd bought to try and grow some more fresh vegetables for the young children were rotten, swimming in a pool of green water. Even the three bottles of whiskey his family sent him as a gift were contaminated and written off. It was heart-breaking to see a grown man break down, holding wads of mushy tea bags and soaked tobacco pouches in his stained hands. We gave him some time to compose himself and when he eventually did, I promised him every teabag on our boat.

He cracked a smile, 'you're too kind,' and in typical island hospitality he offered us all he had left, the last half of a two-litre bottle of coke. We all sat down with him and took a few sips of cola as we tried to cheer him up. It amazes me how people, overcome by adversity, can still be kind and generous with what little they have left.

'Chin up young fellow,' Bob barked, 'it's Bill's birthday today, there'll be plenty for you to eat and drink at the party tonight.'

This encapsulated the whole ethos of Palmerston's community spirit.

We left Derek to the last of his tears and proceeded on our way and Bob explained the hardships of living on such a small island as he showed us around the school.

'Mama Aka, the oldest woman on the island and over ninety, needed to see the dentist. It took her four days to get to Rarotonga and after a quick filling, over six months to get back,' he roared with laughter.

Bob got a little more serious, 'it's not so funny when the cyclones come through though. When the waves get too big our little reef can't protect us, so we strap ourselves and all the children to the coconut trees and pray to God that nobody gets blown away.'

'You tie yourselves to coconut trees?' I asked in amazement.

'Yes,' he said, 'the island is only a metre above sea level, so we have no protective bunkers or cellars to hide in. After the last big storm about a decade ago a handful of people were never seen again.'

I wanted to know more but Bob moved us on, 'I can show you Main Street and the church later, but we need to visit the supply ship before all the good stuff is gone,' he chuckled.

We made our way back through the reef on Bob's little boat and motored out to the deep water where the supply ship was moored.

Palmerston's cash 'crop' was the abundant parrot fish found all over the reefs. Considered a delicacy, the fish were frozen and sent with the supply ship on its return to Tahiti. How long the fish stocks will last is anyone's guess, but when I was there everyone on the island was flush with cash from fishing and the traders were doing a roaring business. They exchanged the frozen fish for bags of frozen New Zealand lamb chops, pots and pans, tobacco and spirits. In fact, there was a glut of supplies on the ship: a moped, textbooks, kid's toys, fishing gear and clothes. There were disposable nappies, soap, sun cream and boxes of soy sauce. Imagine an entire shopping centre all crammed into the rusty hulk of a converted fishing trawler and you'll get the picture. Like a bottomless pit, more and more things for sale kept pouring out of the holds, to the delight of everyone. It was a real fiesta atmosphere and everyone was happy.

Sheila and I were having such a great time that we asked Bob if we could rent some accommodation ashore for the evening. He scoffed, pointedly reminding us we were his adopted family and this meant we'd be staying in his family home.

I protested but he wouldn't have it. Little did I know at the time, but Bob and his wife vacated their bedroom for our convenience and slept on the couch. They'd have literally given the shirts off their backs to help us - the most genuine hospitality from complete strangers I've ever had the privilege of experiencing.

That evening was Bob's cousin Bill's fiftieth birthday party and we were invited to the festivities. Bob also told us to pack some smart clothes for the Sunday church service the next morning.

We swung by Wanderlust to let Harry know we weren't sleeping on board that night, grabbed our gear and Bob took us back ashore as the sun set. After dropping our stuff at Bob's, it was straight to Bill's house to party. I'm not a small guy but I was dwarfed by those island monsters. Most of their arms were bigger than my legs and they could drink! The alcohol bought from the supply ship that day was all consumed in one sitting, with everyone sharing whatever they had. All we could offer was a litre of pink vodka, which didn't last long. The alcohol quickly loosened tongues and it was fascinating to hear the islanders' life stories.

Most of them had grown bored and headed off to New Zealand in their teens, like moths to the city lights, but they'd become disheartened working dead end-jobs and living on the breadline and they'd come to realise that their ancestral island provided them with all they needed to be happy and raise their families in peace. One by one, they'd all eventually returned to be fishermen or teaching assistants, all married beautiful women and fathered a ton of adorable little kids. It was an incredible night filled with the hopes, dreams and fears of some of the most generous people I've ever met.

By midnight, the birthday boy was stinking drunk and started to get boisterous, taking a shine to Sheila's striking blond looks. After some great banter and a rowdy bidding war, the final offer in exchange for 'my wife' was Bill's fishing boat and a spare freezer. I politely declined the offer, pointing out that Sheila was a high-powered businesswoman and would negotiate her own terms. And if I didn't shape up soon, I'd be the one getting sold off for some five-year-old fishing gut, which she'd most likely string me up with afterwards. After a series of brutal, back breaking bear hugs and final well wishes, Sheila and I stumbled back to Bob's house in the early hours, falling asleep to the soothing sound of rustling palms.

There was no rest for the wicked as we were woken at sunrise by a cockerel's relentless crowing. After a quick breakfast everybody dressed in their Sunday best – which for everyone on the island meant bright Hawaiian print shirts - and we walked fifty metres down the sandy strip of Main Street to the church. Greeted by sheepish grins and hungover smiles from a large portion of the congregation, we made our way into the splendid little church. It was a simple structure just big enough to accommodate the whole island's population, adorned with beautiful wood carvings and shell sculptures. The minister, with a knowing smile and a wink, gave Sheila and me a hearty welcome and blessed us for the rest of our voyage. Our blessing was followed by a scripture or two and then a most unexpected and beautiful thing happened.

The drunken demons from the previous night's festivities transformed into euphoric angels as they simultaneously sang interwoven melodies with the rest of the congregation. Their baritone voices perfectly accompanied the higher pitched female voices of their wives in a stunning melodic counterpoint. The virtuous sounds of Polynesian polyphonic singing filled the church and my heart and soul soared. Their songs ebbed and flowed like the ocean surrounding them, never losing balance, rolling back and forth like the unstoppable tides that maintained the rhythm of life on the beautiful atoll they called home. It sounded to me like centuries of memories collected by those who spent their entire lives listening to the sea. Somehow, they'd managed to decode the ocean's essence and encapsulated its infinite beauty in song. My eyes moistened as wave after wave of those incredible voices rolled over me. As I looked out through the window of the church - so central to these beautiful people's souls - my eyes settled on a pristine white sandy beach, surrounded by the most beautiful blue of an ocean framed by the effervescent green of life giving coconut trees, and while I listened to the most ethereal music I'd ever heard I could see why my new friends had lost heart with the modern world and returned to their ancestral home. Whatever strife and struggle were occurring elsewhere on earth, on that perfect Sunday morning in Palmerston, there was only peace and tranquillity.

After some emotional farewells and another round of back breaking man-hugs outside the church, we collected our gear and made our way down to the water. As Bob took us 'home' I looked back towards the island and reflected on how lucky I was to experience such a unique place and its people, one of only a handful of guests who would ever have the privilege. We waved our goodbyes to Bob and his little tribe from the safety of our yacht as they threaded their way back through the reef, back to their home, that magnificent little pearl in the middle of the Pacific.

Bob Marsters and his family on Palmerston Main Street

Chapter 13

Niue, Tonga and Fiji

18-19ºS, 169ºW-178E

After our enchanting time in Palmerston we made a quick stop in Niue. I'd never even heard of the island beforehand and I had no idea what to expect. Affectionally referred to as 'The Rock' by the locals, Niue is one of the smallest nations but also one of the largest raised coral islands to be found anywhere in the world. With no natural harbour to provide protection from the ocean's waves or any accommodating beaches, the islanders have an ingenious method of getting sailors ashore. On the concrete quay there is an electric crane which you hook onto your tender. Once it's securely fastened you lift your little boat clear of the water and out of the pounding waves, swing it ashore and then lower the tender onto a little metal trailer provided by the dock master, wheel it away from the water's edge and park it safely in the dinghy parking lot on the dock. A brilliant solution to overcome the challenging swell.

With only a couple of days ashore, Sheila and I rented a scooter with which to explore the island. Niue's steep limestone cliffs have been eroded to create some stunning structures, so our first stop was the island's most famous natural phenomena, the Tavala arch.

Tavala Arch

After parking the moped, we followed a well-worn track through a verdant tropical forest overflowing with luscious shrubs and ferns. With the help of some static ropes we scrambled over the razor-sharp rock and through an intricate cave system, heading downwards towards the sound of crashing waves. The noise of the waves below us was rather unnerving as it was strangely amplified by the cavernous interior of the underground chambers. We emerged from the gloomy caves to the incredible sight of a heart shaped arch perfectly framing the Tavala arch about fifty metres out to sea. Tavala's thick and rather stocky looking arch spanned forty metres of an ocean sparkling like a million gleaming diamonds; some of the cleanest saltwater to be found anywhere in the world.

The incredible underwater visibility of around seventy metres is due to the fact that there are no streams, rivers or lakes anywhere on the island. The entire land mass is made up of porous limestone and any rainwater that falls, filters directly through the rock, resulting in zero runoff with not an ounce of silt in the surrounding sea. It makes for an incredible place to dive on the one condition that you're not scared of snakes. Around the coastal waters of Niue, there are tens of thousands of coral sea snakes, a species of banded sea kraits known as Katuali. A highly venomous relative of the cobra, their bite is ten times more lethal than a rattlesnake's. The locals told me not to worry about them as they're generally not aggressive, but they still gave me one hell of a shock when they swam directly towards me from the depths below. The Katuali were only heading to the surface to breathe but they still nearly caused me to foul the water clarity on numerous occasions.

The whole coastline of Niue is littered with grottos and stunning natural swimming pools which we had all to ourselves. With a population of one-thousand-five-hundred people and only two flights to the island a week, there were so few people around it was a welcome change to see the occasional visitor as we scrambled through countless caves and rock pools. In one of those sunken chasms we found the natural swimming baths exclusively reserved for the island's royalty a century before. With sheer cliff walls reflecting the sparkling, multi-coloured coral below and crystal-clear waters teeming with sea life, it felt like I was swimming in my own private aquarium. Niue is a unique gem, perched on its own in the middle of an ocean and the perfect place to escape to if you love a little solitude.

My time with Sheila was drawing to a close but we still had one more circumnavigation milestone to complete together as we set sail for Tonga. The international date line runs between Niue and Tonga and as we crossed it the local time changed from -11 UTC to +13 UTC. The planet, being a circle, is split into three hundred and sixty longitudinal meridians which run from the north to south poles. With twenty-four hours in a day, for every fifteen degrees you travel east or west you lose or gain an hour. We'd travelled west for almost half the world, constantly turning the clocks back and gaining an hour each time, but those hours don't come for free. As we crossed the international date line, we jumped from a Sunday straight to a Tuesday, missing out Monday the 6th of June 2016. It was no great loss though; nobody likes Mondays anyway!

It was a short two-day crossing before we arrived in Tonga and thankfully my last voyage with Harry aboard Wanderlust. It was kind of him to take Sheila and me onboard, but relations between the two of us were extremely strained and it was high time I left him to his own devices. Massimo and his boat Giampi had arrived in Tonga a week before us and he was raring to get going again. Massimo didn't plan on heading to

Indonesia, where Sheila needed to get to in order to finish her circumnavigation, so sadly she couldn't accompany me any further. In between transferring my gear from Wanderlust to Giampi, I spent the rest of my time trying to secure Sheila a berth on another yacht. After all we'd been through on Wanderlust I had zero confidence in Harry's skippering abilities. Without personally being onboard to oversee his decisions, I had many sleepless nights worrying about Sheila's future safety. I'd spoken to everyone in the fleet, but all the other boats were full, and I was close to despair. For our last couple of days together Sheila and I rented a little hotel room ashore. While she was getting ready for our last night out on the town, I thought I'd pop out for a quick pint and give it one final try. A very fortuitous decision indeed as I immediately bumped into my dear friends Emma and Andy, a salt of the earth British couple and proper drinkers like me. They were chatting to a rather hippy looking couple who'd just sailed in.

'Evening all, who needs a beer?' I asked.

'We'll never say no,' Andy said and Emma gestured the thumbs up sign.

Andy wrapped his arm around my shoulder, 'Daz, meet Brian and Kym, brand new arrivals to the wonderful Kingdom of Tonga.'

We exchanged the usual pleasantries and I toddled off to the bar.

On my return Brian asked, 'Andy says you've only recently arrived but you're setting sail tomorrow. Not sticking around for a while?'

'Sadly not,' I said, 'I'd love to explore these islands but there isn't time. I've just jumped ship from a god-awful skipper to my mate's boat, and he's got a deadline to meet back in Europe. We have to get a move on if we're going to make it back in time.'

I looked at Andy again, 'are you sure you can't squeeze one more person onto your boat?'

'Sorry bud,' he said, 'as I told you yesterday and the day before that, the only berth we have spare is in the forepeak and it's jammed full of sails. There's only enough space for the two of us aboard Pentagram.'

'Bollocks, I'm all out of options then!'

'Sorry, I'm a bit confused Daz,' Kym interjected, 'I thought you just said you had a new boat already.'

'Oh, it's not for me. It's for my girlfriend, Sheila.'

Over a couple of beers and a game of pool I explained Sheila's predicament and relayed my fears.

'Well, we'd love to help out, but we are only heading as far west as Fiji. I'm a retired doctor and Kym and I are sailing over to Fiji to provide humanitarian aid in the wake of the recent cyclone. If Sheila joined our boat she'd be months behind you.'

'Anything would be better than her current situation,' I replied, 'and as things stand, I am forging ahead to finish my circumnavigation. The earliest I'd see Sheila again anyway would be once that's completed in six months' time.'

'Well, if she isn't in a rush and we like her, I guess we could use the help.'

Sheila arrived soon afterwards and they were captivated by her, just like I had been when I first set eyes on her in St Lucia, half a world away. By the end of the evening she had a new berth and I sighed with relief, my final parting gift to a brave and beautiful woman. We'd both known for months that our time together was drawing to a close, but that didn't make it any easier to part ways. I was extremely fortunate to have had such an adventurous wing woman whose love of the ocean matched mine. Circumstances aboard Wanderlust may not have been ideal and living together in such close confines was a challenge in itself, but we had loads of fun anyway and I'm thankful that Sheila was such a big part of my trip. Both of our futures were in flux, with no idea when we'd next see each other, but such is the life of a sailor. I'd miss her over the upcoming months but I'd known, ever since giving up May, that there'd be a huge emotional price to pay if I was ever going to succeed on my quest to sail around the world. The next morning, after a subdued breakfast, we walked hand in hand down to the dock and said our emotional farewells. I jumped into Massimo's tender and waved goodbye as Sheila slowly faded into the distance.

Heartbreak aside, moving onto Giampi was amazing. For the first time on the whole trip I was finally sailing on a yacht with a skipper I respected and completely trusted. Massimo is one of the most genuine, intelligent and interesting guys I've ever met. With a shared passion for fishing and free diving, we got on right from the start, and he'd become my confidant and sounding board whenever I needed advice. The story of his circumnavigation is a sad yet uplifting one and worth the telling so you can get a small glimpse into the quality of the man.

Massimo's father, a customs official in the Italian port of Carrara (where the marble for Michelangelo's statues came from), had always said he wanted to sail around the world, but retirement loomed and he'd never got around to it. Massimo, a doting and devoted son, sold his company and bought Giampi, which he named after his only brother who had tragically died in a car crash. His goal had always been to take his father around the world, selflessly making his dream come true. With his mum, his dad and Giampi, they set off from Europe and crossed the North Atlantic. Neither of his parents had ever done any serious sailing before and the ocean crossing was their second honeymoon, but tragedy struck. On their arrival in the Caribbean, Massimo's father fell ill and was flown back to Italy where he sadly passed away a few weeks later. When I heard the story, it was just another stark reminder that life is too short, nobody knows what's around the next corner and you have to seize the moment and make your dreams a reality.

This was his second circumnavigation attempt, but his trials and tribulations weren't over yet. His sister had subsequently fallen ill back in Italy so he decided to leave the WARC and head home - via the Cape of Good Hope on the southern tip of South Africa. He made his future plans clear to me when he'd offered me a spot on his boat after our chat in the Galapagos and they suited me perfectly. My primary objective was to circumnavigate the globe by sail, but an addendum to that goal was also to sail back via the country of my birth, South Africa. With both our goals aligned, it was a match made in heaven.

The rest of the motley crew on Giampi consisted of Ralf, a stocky red headed East German who's very proud of his eastern bloc heritage, and Michelino, a piratical looking character with wild hair and piercings who's an undertaker by profession. We were a happy crew of misfits and set off together for Fiji.

Our first stop in Fiji was the decimated district of Lomaloma on Vanua Balavu. We arrived four months after tropical cyclone Winston passed directly over the island and destroyed everything in its path. An automatic weather station ashore recorded a mean wind speed of 233 km/h and a final gust of 306km/h before it went offline, ripped away by the highest wind speed ever recorded in Fiji. The cyclone was so strong it tore the channel markers from the reef.

'I have no idea where the channel is, guys,' Massimo said on arrival, 'keep a wary eye out as I'll have to follow the electronic charts.'

At first, all went well as we inched our way towards the shoreline with Michelino and me scanning the reassuringly dark blue water ahead, but all the blue suddenly gave away to an ominous grey.

'Back!' We both screamed in unison as Massimo slammed the engine in reverse and we stopped a metre short of a solid wall of jagged reef.

'*Fanculo,*' we heard Massimo shout in reply, 'the charts are wrong!'

We saw a couple of locals on the shore waving their arms in warning and seconds later the VHF radio crackled into life.

'Sailing vessel approaching Lomaloma. Do you copy? Over.'

'Yes, we copy,' Massimo replied. 'Over.'

'The satellite navigation charts are inaccurate for this area. You need to head south for approximately one hundred metres then head directly to shore to make it through the channel. Over.'

Another sailor, anchored in the safety of the bay, had seen our predicament and helped out. The unwritten rule of the brotherhood of blue water cruisers. We always have each other's backs.

'Roger, thanks for the assistance, out.'

We backed up into deeper water, followed the directions south and spotted the welcome sight of white sand under our keel and a clear run through the channel into the protected waters behind the reef. It was a close call and it just goes to show that when there's coral reef about, don't trust anything other than your lookouts' eyes. Once we'd anchored, we went ashore and I've never seen such carnage. The devastation was unbelievable, with bridges and roads washed away by the storm surge. Some of the houses were scoured down to their foundations with only the toilet bowl still attached to the floor. Roofs were ripped off, trees uprooted, and huge piles of debris were everywhere. Even the coconut palms, evolved to withstand hurricane force winds, were totally stripped of leaves if they were still upright at all. Yet, despite the death, destruction and complete mayhem, the people of Lomaloma were still walking around with wide smiles on their faces. They were the happiest islanders I've met anywhere on my travels and the constant greeting of 'Bula Bula' followed us everywhere we went.

After surveying the damage, we made our way over to a UNICEF tent where a temporary primary school was set up. Once again it was all smiles and a cacophony of laughing children. To have lost everything, but still remain so infectiously positive, was a real testament to the resilience of the human spirit. We spent the rest of the day playing with the kids before heading back out through the channel the next morning, following our GPS inward track to within a metre, making sure we didn't come a cropper on the unmarked reef.

An equally disturbing vista greeted our arrival in Suva on the south eastern tip of Viti Levu, Fiji's main island. Stacked together on mooring buoys, twenty-five deep, was a large Chinese fishing fleet preparing to head out to sea and further decimate the once abundant tuna stocks of the region. Each boat could take up to a hundred tons of fish at a time, and they were only one of the many international fleets plying their trade in those waters. For a short-term gain that'll have extreme long-term consequences, the Fijian government sold off their territorial fishing rights to foreign countries, destroying their domestic fishing operations in the process. Another example of a beautiful country selling its soul to the devil, allowing its natural resources to be stripped through pure, unadulterated greed. I watched with dismay as the Chinese sailors prepared their ships for sea and thought of the island's fishermen and their families who had no say in the matter. How is it possible that, on the same planet, there are some people with so little but who are infinitely happy, and others who have everything they could ever possibly need but still take more? We live in a world where the affluent are dying of obesity yet the poor are starving to death. I find the disparity between these two opposite ends of the spectrum incomprehensible.

We spent a couple of days in Suva, exploring the local town and doing a few repairs to the boat. Sadly, Michelino's time on board was up and he returned to Spain to be with his daughter. He had sailed halfway around the world with Massimo and we'd all miss him very much. Although he spoke little English and I spoke even less Spanish, we nevertheless formed a firm friendship, thoroughly enjoying each other's presence in a companionable silence. I guess it was a skill he had plenty of practice perfecting in his job as an undertaker.

Fiji had one final surprise in store for me. One morning back in Niue I'd befriended a man called Pato - Everaldo 'Pato' Teixeira to be exact - when we helped each other crane our tenders ashore. *Pato* - the Portuguese word for duck - is a world famous Brazilian professional surfer. He was sailing around the South Pacific to film the next season of his family's sail and surf odyssey and with a joint love of all things to do with the ocean we got on well. Pato and I had repeatedly bumped into each other over the following weeks until, in Suva, he invited me to go surfing with him and his camera crew on a film shoot. With just the two of us in the water, we had great fun on a little reef break, and it was a real honour to share some waves with somebody so prodigiously talented. One of the beautiful things about sailing around the world is that you never know just who you might meet and what adventures are around the next corner.

Chapter 14

The ring of fire

19°31'45S, 169°29'45E

Our time in Fiji came to an end all too quickly. With one less crew member we sailed away from Suva and while I watched the land gradually disappear, I vowed I'd return one day to explore the three hundred islands and surf to my heart's content.

The next country on our route to Australia was the Republic of Vanuatu. Although we were sailing to a tight schedule, I managed to persuade Massimo to make an unscheduled stop in Tanna, one of the eighty-three islands making up the archipelago. Famous for having one of the most accessible active volcanoes in the world, I didn't want to miss out on the opportunity of a lifetime to experience the planet's primordial power first-hand.

About two days out from Tanna, Massimo and I were both trawling with our fishing rods on a calm, quiet, and beautiful sailing day when suddenly, both reels started to scream at the same time. We sprinted to the stern and grabbed a rod each in an attempt to slow down the two beasts that had taken our lures, shouting at Ralf to stop the boat.

Massimo's fun didn't last long. He cursed a couple of minutes later as his fish snapped him off but I was luckier and managed to slow mine down and turn it before running out of line. Little did I know that I was in for another monumental three-hour long battle as I fought one of the most powerful predators in the ocean. Drawing on the experience I'd gained while fighting Bob Marlin, I played the long game, reeling in some line and then releasing it again when the fish took off on another headlong dive into the depths. Back and forth the pendulum swung, but as the hours ticked by, I gained the upper hand and the fish began to tire. With my arm and back muscles screaming in agony, I finally managed to get the monster near the surface, and it was an astonishing sight. On the end of my line was a giant silver torpedo, weighing in somewhere around the hundred-kilogram mark, the biggest yellow fin tuna I've ever seen. It was so big we wondered if we'd be able to get it through the swim platform's companionway and onto the boat, but that certainly wasn't going to stop us trying to haul it aboard. I hand lined the fish the last five metres, just like I'd done with the marlin, and Massimo, cramped for space with the two of us on the tiny swim platform, narrowly missed spearing the beast on his first attempt. Spooked, the monstrous tuna took off again. I scrambled back into the cockpit and grabbed the rod I'd given to Ralf and the battle started anew. After another half hour of fighting, I once again turned the fish and pulled it around for Massimo's second attempt to spear it. He leaned over, spear held high and the titan somehow sensed that that was its one and only chance of survival, flicked its tale in a last ditch attempt to evade capture, shot underneath the boat and snapped my line.

'Fuck! Fuck! Fuck!' I bellowed, heartbroken as I watched the massive silver bullet disappear back into the depths. After such a titanic struggle I collapsed from fatigue, feeling so dejected about losing that once-in-a-lifetime catch that I barely spoke for the rest of the day. I could have kicked myself. I'd been so wrapped up in the fight I'd totally forgotten that Massimo had a spear gun on board which would have made the final kill a mere formality. The disappointment on the boat was palpable and to this day I can still remember all the scenarios whizzing through my mind afterwards of what we should have done to land the monster. Sometimes it just isn't meant to be and that's the one fish I'll always remember that managed to get away.

My melancholy mood only lasted a day and I was back to being my excitable self. As we approached Tanna, there looked to be a giant, low lying cloud over the southern part of the island. It became evident that this was in fact a huge plume of smoke that constantly billows up from the volcano. Once we got to within a few miles of land, we saw flashes of light reflected on its underside, and as night began to fall the smoke cloud took on an eerie red glow, overshadowing the whole mountain. It was a rather sinister spectacle.

We anchored up in Port Resolution that evening and were soon visited by two French brothers in their sixties, André and Claude, who popped aboard for a beer. They had spotted that we were sailing a Wauquiez yacht, a famous French designed boat and the same make as theirs. You don't see too many of them around and the owners are like an old boys' club, so they came straight over to investigate. As we crushed a dozen beers, they gave us tons of local information about the island and offered to pick us up early in the morning to watch a football match. We assumed at first it was a local football game, but it turned out France were playing the Republic of Ireland in the European Championships and it was being televised at the local primary school.

Always up for new experiences, we readily agreed to join them at first light. With such knowledgeable chaps aboard, we enquired about customs and immigration. We hadn't planned on stopping in Tanna so we were taking a bit of a chance with the island's authorities. As mentioned previously, for almost all the islands in the South Pacific you need to register your intention of visiting prior to arrival. We hadn't registered, but as we only planned to stay for a couple of days, we hoped we could get away with it. The brothers agreed it shouldn't be a problem for us as the authority's offices were on the other side of the island and it was unlikely they knew we'd arrived.

The next morning André and Claude picked us up and took us ashore. We met up with the crew from another French boat, scrambled up a steep bank and wandered over to the only brick building in sight. We were welcomed by the school's headmaster, and for a Dollar admission fee, we headed into the school hall which was packed to the rafters. There were over a hundred people squeezed into the room, spanning six generations, with every soul in the village present.

Most of them wore an outrageous mix of different football kits and sporting attire in varying degrees of disrepair and all screamed from their benches at a tiny little television perched on a stool at the front of the room. The animated locals hustled up to let us squeeze in and it was game on.

I couldn't make out where the ball was on the grainy television picture, but the atmosphere was electric as the crowd 'OOOHD' and 'AAAHD' at every move. It was surreal to sit in a tiny little village in Vanuatu, watching the satellite footage of a football game being played on the other side of the planet, with a bunch of French sailors and a howling mob of excited Pacific islanders. It just goes to show that football truly is the global game. In the end France won 2-1, to the delight of our new sailing friends and to the dismay of our hosts. Living on an island, they felt it was their patriotic duty to shout for Ireland, the underdogs, as well as hoping to see their old colonial overseers lose.

After showing us around his village the headmaster booked us onto a volcano tour that evening. With a few hours to kill we decided to explore the island by 4x4 taxi truck. We all jumped in and proceeded to get bounced around on possibly the worst road in the world. About half an hour into the back-breaking trip, we were flagged down by an oncoming truck. The vehicle was brand new, looked very official and the driver was the first person on the island I'd seen with a crisp white shirt and no smile. Mr Customs had found us and he didn't look happy.

'You must be the fellas who arrived last night. Where do you think you're going?' Mr Customs enquired with a snarl.

'Good morning sir,' Massimo replied without skipping a beat, 'we're heading directly to your office in Lenakel to check in, of course. Where are you heading?'

Massimo, being a quick thinker and a resourceful chap, had brought along the ship's papers and our passports, just in case.

'Where I go is none of your concern. You're illegally on my island.'

'Well, as I just stated, our taxi driver is delivering us to your office. Will one of your colleagues be available to help us when we get there?' Massimo asked as if butter wouldn't melt in his mouth.

'I am the only customs official on this island,' he said pompously, 'report to my office at two o'clock sharp as I have other official business to attend to beforehand.'

'Probably his lunch, the fat bastard,' I whispered in Ralf's ear as he valiantly fought the urge to burst out laughing.

The official looked on unimpressed, somehow sensing he'd been the butt of a joke.

'Two o'clock it is then, have a wonderful day sir... ciao,' Massimo waved, as Mr Customs spun his wheels and sped off in a cloud of smoke and dust.

'What a delightful gentleman,' I commented, 'this is certainly shaping up to be an entertaining afternoon.'

After passing through dense jungle the terrain changed markedly to one of a barren moonscape. Miles upon miles of grey ash blanketed everything in sight. Except for a few tenacious weeds and a toxic looking stream we crossed, nothing else moved. We were on the suffocated plains below Mount Yasur, a volcano that's erupted continuously for hundreds of years. After the green, lush and brightly lit forest, the grey, dead and overcast wasteland felt very ominous indeed.

After a couple of bouncy hours squashed into our 'private' taxi - our driver picked up all and sundry and crammed them in like sardines - we arrived in Lenakel, Tanna's capital on the opposite side of the island. With a long voyage to Australia ahead we took advantage of the huge fresh produce market in the centre of the town and stocked up for the journey. Everything was available - from staples like taro, yams and sweet potatoes to fruit I'd never seen before. There were huge jackfruit that taste like a combination of pineapple and mango. Sweetsop and soursop had a strange, almost snotty texture but reminded me of a delicious medley of tropical fruits. Then there was breadfruit. It wasn't much like a fruit but as its name implies, once it's cooked it has the smell and consistency of freshly baked bread. It was great fun bartering with the super friendly Tannese natives, but the produce was so cheap none of us tried very hard. I'm always happy to pay a little over the odds in remote places like Vanuatu. The minuscule amount of money I'd save meant a whole lot more to the local population than it ever would to me.

With our shopping done and the dusty, crumbling town centre explored, the three of us marched over to the government building at two o'clock sharp to await our fate. The immigration officer, resplendent in a beautifully colourful kaftan, cheerfully greeted us and welcomed us to Vanuatu. After a cursory glance at our papers he checked us in and out of the country at the same time, stamped our passports and wished us a safe but exciting trip up to the volcano. So far so good as I wondered what I'd been worrying about. I was soon to find out. We walked next door to the customs officer and he wasn't smiling. He'd driven all the way to Port Resolution that morning to check in another yacht who'd notified him in advance of their arrival and he was furious that he'd caught us attempting to enter the country illegally. He stated that the fine was 250USD for the boat and 50USD per person and we must leave the island immediately. Massimo, completely unfazed by the customs official's outburst, put on an Oscar winning performance, and talked our way out of the fix we'd found ourselves in.

At first he implored and cajoled the official, to no effect. Then Massimo attempted reasoning with him, but to no avail. Finally, after trying almost every trick in the book and waving his hands around like an Italian mob boss commanding a hit, he changed tactic and threatened dire repercussions for the island's tourism industry if we got fined and thrown out. Somehow, he managed to get on the phone with the head of customs for the whole country and argued with him for an age. After a relentless two-hour verbal barrage, Massimo gradually turned the tables and the poor customs official was totally brow beaten. In the end his commanding officer berated him, ordered him to let us stay to shut Massimo up and agreed that we'd only have to pay the standard 50USD cruising permit. Massimo handed over a crisp fifty, requested a receipt and sauntered back to the truck grinning like a Cheshire Cat, pleased as punch with his own performance. I still can't believe how he managed to turn the situation around.

It was getting late so we headed back the way we'd come, straight to the foot of the volcano. We were quickly ushered through the visitors centre and bundled into the back of another 4x4, the last guests to arrive for the evening tour due to Massimo's prolonged negotiations. Our driver must have been the local rally car racer and he flew up the side of the mountain, narrowly missing tree trunks while overhead branches thumped into the roof and we slammed into each other and were thrown from side to side as he negotiated the sharp bends. It was brilliant and my heart was racing by the time he slammed on the brakes and we screeched to a halt. We all jumped out and our waiting guide gave a us a quick safety briefing.

By quick I mean it was literally, 'stay behind me,' and that was it.

Health and safety didn't seem high on the agenda even though we'd heard that several people's lives had been prematurely extinguished by the volcano in recent years. The guide didn't seem overly anxious though, so I set off with a spring in my step, but as we ascended a well-trodden path up the mountain, I was beginning to feel more and more unsettled. I couldn't quite place what was making me feel so uneasy until I realised the ground underfoot was vibrating, imperceptibly at first, but intensifying with each step I took. Buried deep in my subconscious and most likely imbedded in my very DNA, was a little voice telling me to run, to turn tail and get the fuck out of there. I'd only ever felt that deep well of fear and impending doom once – in New Zealand, seconds before I experienced my first earthquake. The whole world had gone haywire and it felt like I was about to get run over by a freight train as the earth shook violently from side to side beneath me.

When living on a boat you become completely attuned to your environment and every cell in my body was screaming that there was something terribly wrong with the surroundings I found myself in. As I marched up the mountain, I experienced a mounting sense of dread as all my senses went into overdrive. The earth began to shake more violently the higher we went, accompanied by a muffled, guttural rumble. As we approached the summit, a massive eruption sprayed molten lava into the night sky like fireworks and I gazed up with a mixture of fear and sheer astonishment. It took all my will power to keep one foot moving in front of the other as I walked fifty metres across the plateau. Finally, we approached the caldera's lip, four hundred metres in diameter and close to a perfect circle. One minute the ground was flat and then it just fell away at a steep gradient to the fire and brimstone below. Without a single guard rail in sight, any slip or misstep meant one last short ride to a warm reception in hell.

Looking down into that pit of doom was like staring into the maw of a terrifying beast. A hundred metres below me was a constantly boiling cauldron of fiery fury, violently spluttering away like a huge pan of super-heated oil. The night sky was pitch black so I could clearly see the molten rock bubbling below, as if the Devil was boiling a huge pan of blazing blood in the volcano. Then BOOM! A huge eruption of incandescent volcanic rock and lava bombs were propelled hundreds of metres into the air as the volcano released some pressure from the immense power raging below our feet. A millisecond later the percussion of a thousand canons, all fired at the same time, made my heart skip a beat. Seconds later I was buffeted by a scorching wind and then finally showered with a hail of black ash as sharp as glass, clawing its way into every available orifice, scratching my eyes, scraping my throat and burrowing its way into my ears, letting me know in no uncertain terms that I was trespassing in a place where I was not welcome.

After each eruption, massive globules of lava - some the size of cars - spun through the air and spread out in beautiful arcs, like a fan. It was reminiscent of a huge, coloured water fountain, the only difference being that it was a thousand degrees hotter. The lava's vertical trajectory stalled in the air for a split second before plummeting back down to earth, perceptively changing brightness as it fell and exploded on impact with the solid rock on the crater's edge in a final display of brilliance. Then it gradually faded away as it cooled, turning from a liquid to a solid in a matter of seconds. I couldn't believe that it was rock, the solid base of the planet I took for granted. The amount of furious energy billowing up from beneath was staggering. Standing on the edge of the caldera was like watching the birth of our world and I was overwhelmed by the volcano's primordial power. In a thousand-degree heat a human being would be atomised in an instant and although it was terrifying, I knew I was witnessing how life on our planet first began billions of years before mankind was even an itch in the universe's ball sack.

It was a mind-blowing experience to get a tiny glimpse of the unfathomable power of nature and how those forces moulded our incredible planet. Nowhere else had ever made me feel so humble, and to be perfectly frank, so insignificant and scared. I'd felt tiny in the middle of the Pacific Ocean, but Mount Yasur showed me how truly inconsequential my existence is. At least in the middle of the ocean I had a chance to survive whatever was thrown at me, but standing on the edge of that volcano, bearing witness to only a fraction of its potential explosive force, I knew that I was truly out of my depth. After a quarter of an hour the overwhelming feeling of dread I'd initially felt had dissipated into an uncomfortable one of simmering foreboding, yet it was impossible to tear my eyes away from that primal pyrotechnic display of pure power. I spent over an hour gazing in wonder as explosion after explosion shook the world, shaking the very foundations of the earth itself. By the time we left I was completely covered in ash; black from head to toe. It took weeks to rid myself of all that piercing grit, but the vision of its exploding volcanic birthplace will be forever seared into my soul.

A Ni-Vanuatu fisherman in his dugout canoe

Chapter 15

Australian walkabout

12°27'00S, 130°5100E

After waving goodbye to all the friends we'd made during our two day stay in Port Resolution, the three of us settled in for the two and a half thousand-nautical-mile journey to Darwin which we estimated would take three weeks.

Darwin is located in the centre of the north coast of Australia and from Vanuatu it's the distance of another Atlantic crossing, but with one major difference. Between the two stands the world's biggest reef and one of the most notorious straits in the world, but we had a week of open ocean to cover first so we ensconced ourselves in the daily routine of sailing, relaxing and enjoying each other's company. With all my free time spent lounging in the cockpit, either reading or chatting with Massimo and Ralf, they were halcyon days of sun kissed bliss. One of the wonderful things about sailing, especially cruising around the world, was the quality of the other sailors I got to spend my time with. Most of them were successful in their own field of expertise, with varied life experiences from which to draw their wisdom.

One evening, about five days into the voyage, we were all enjoying a beer while we watched a beautiful sunset from the back of the boat. I was talking about traveling and had been going on for some time when Massimo interrupted me.

'Daz, I am going to have to stop you there.'

He'd been looking a little bemused for a while and I could sense he'd been mulling something over in his mind. I stopped talking. He then gave me one of the best pieces of interpersonal communications advice I've ever been given.

'Have you ever heard of the rule of three I's?' he enquired.

'Erm, nope. I can't say I have.'

'I thought not. Well it's a simple rule and goes as follows. When you hear yourself starting three consecutive sentences with the word 'I', it's time for you to shut the fuck up and ask somebody else a question.'

'What do you mean mate?' I asked rather taken aback.

'Exactly that,' he replied, 'now we are having a conversation again. You've asked me a question and I answered you.'

Massimo went on to clarify the rule.

'When you're constantly talking about yourself, people lose interest a whole lot quicker than you'd imagine. As interesting as you think you are, unless your audience gets an opportunity to contribute to the conversation, they'll get bored of your company, switch off and then you may as well be talking to the sea,' he finished with a chuckle.

That piece of advice improved my communication skills immensely and highlighted to me that the people I find most interesting tend to be interested in me.

The Great Barrier Reef stretches for 2300 kilometres along the East Coast of Australia. It's the world's biggest single structure made by living organisms and can be seen from outer space. After a week of relaxed sailing in open ocean, tension began to rise as we drew closer.

'I don't like the look of this,' Massimo mumbled as he surveyed the charts, 'there's reef everywhere.'

All of our experience with reefs up to that point had been tinged with a certain amount of anxiety. First, they weren't always where the charts said they were supposed to be and second, in the South Pacific they weren't all marked.

'But we've timed it perfectly boys,' Massimo stated with confidence, 'there's a few hours of daylight left and I've found a perfect spot to anchor up for the night once we're through.'

We had no idea what to expect, but within a few hours of safely negotiating the wide gap in the reef, half a dozen cargo ships passed us in the channel and it became clear that there wasn't much to worry about from the reef itself. The channel was wide, well-marked and professionally maintained like any other commercial shipping lane. What required vigilance were all the big ships plying their trade in the sheltered waters inside the reef. After a discussion with Massimo we agreed to push on through the night instead of stopping to anchor, and we continued in that vain for the next five days. Except for the occasional flyover from an Australian Customs aeroplane to check our progress it was an incident free transit. Well, incident free with regard to the reef, but not incident free with regard to my future plans for circumnavigating.

Sitting in the cockpit and enjoying a drink together at sunset, as usual, I could see something was bugging Massimo.

'What's up mate, still worried about sailing inside the reef at night?' I poked a bit of fun at him as I took a long cold sip of my beer.

'No, it's not that,' he replied looking rather dejected, 'there is no easy way to say this but here goes. I mulled this over for months, Daz, and I've finally come to a decision.'

This wasn't sounding good and I put my beer down and gave him my full attention.

'I've decided to head back to Europe via the Suez Canal. I know it's not what we discussed when you moved aboard, but I cannot in good conscience take the extra two to three months to sail via Cape Town. With my father gone, my elderly mum trying to run the family business and my sister's health deteriorating, I have to get back to Italy as soon as possible.'

'What about the Somali pirates?' I asked, a little in shock.

Over the past decade there'd been hundreds of attempted hijackings in and around the Indian Ocean and Arabian Sea, making the route untenable for little boats.

'It's a risk I'm willing to take to get back to my family sooner. I'm sorry my friend.'

After the disappointing news that Massimo wasn't sailing via South Africa anymore, I had a huge decision to make. On the one hand I loved the camaraderie and spirit aboard Giampi. Both Massimo and Ralf were great guys and I'd have sailed to the ends of earth with them. For the first time on the whole voyage I truly felt at home, safe and secure with competent sailors. On the other hand, I'd always dreamt of sailing back to the land of my birth and pitting myself against the Cape of Good Hope, the infamous southern tip of Africa and home to some of the most violent storms in the world. I was torn between the option of remaining on board the safe haven of Giampi or risking it all and jumping ship again. It was a tough decision to make but I knew in my heart there could never be a compromise. After a couple of days of introspection, I came to a decision.

'I'm sorry buddy,' I confided in Massimo, 'if I don't sail around the world via South Africa, I know in the future I'll look back on this journey with regret. I won't have completed what I set out to do, and I can't live with that.'

'No my friend. It is not you who needs to apologise. I'm sorry I've changed my plans and let you down.'

'It looks like I'm going to have to find another boat then.' I replied.

After firing up the satellite telephone and sending a quick email he smiled, 'Don't worry. I may have a solution.'

That evening Massimo checked his emails.

'Well, what is it?' I asked when Massimo's face lit up as he read the message.

'I've fixed it my friend,' he exclaimed as he threw his fists in the air.

'Fixed what?'

'Well, this morning I messaged my good friend Miguel, the skipper aboard Aliena. I explained our situation and he just replied. He'd be delighted to have you onboard his yacht for crossing the Indian Ocean.'

Miguel and his wife Carmen, a Spanish couple in their mid-sixties were also a part of the WARC fleet. They were quite reserved in nature, so I knew them but not well.

'But I barely even know them.' I replied

'No problem. I promise you they are very good people. They know you're a good sailor and I've vouched for you. So if you want, you have a boat to continue your circumnavigation from Darwin onwards.'

'Yes, of course I want it,' I shouted in excitement as I jumped up and gave him a big hug, 'you absolute legend!'

After we successfully negotiated the Great Barrier Reef, the next major hurdle was to sail through one of the most dangerous maritime areas in the world - the Torres Strait separating Australia from Papua New Guinea, linking the Coral Sea in the east with the Arafura Sea and the Gulf of Carpentaria to the west. Although it's a major international shipping route, it weaves its way thought a maze of reefs and islands in extremely shallow water. It's also the meeting point of two oceans that have different mean sea level heights due to the difference between their salinities and temperature changes within the water column. During some phases of the moon at certain times of the year, it can be high water at one end of the straight and low water at the other, comparable to using a couple of drinking straws to transfer the water back and forth between two swimming pools. From a tidal perspective, Torres is probably the most complicated area in the world. Captain Matthew Finders, the first man to circumnavigate Australia and identify it as a continent at the beginning of the 19th Century stated, 'Perhaps no space of three and a half degrees in length represents more dangers than Torres Strait.'

Keep in mind that when this was written, cannibalism was rife in the region, so getting the tides wrong and getting shipwrecked was a death sentence.

We planned to shoot through the strait on a favourable tide, as close to sunrise as possible so we could navigate in good light, and many hours were spent pouring over the charts and tide tables. After numerous calculations we slowed the boat down and sailed at six knots for two days on our final approach. The fateful day arrived and we headed early one morning for the Prince of Wales Channel, the safest looking option through the strait. A quick VHF call to a passing freighter confirmed the tide was just about to turn in our favour and our timing was spot on. With twelve hours of daylight ahead of us and a perfect weather forecast, we entered the channel and the strong current whipped us through the strait. Exiting safely on the other side as the tide began to turn again at sundown, it was the prefect transit and we congratulated each other on a job well done.

But King Neptune doesn't like cocky sailors. Even though we'd successfully overcome the two major hurdles of the Great Barrier Reef and Torres Strait, he still had something else up his sleeve. The next morning the beautiful blue skies we'd enjoyed for a fortnight were replaced by black, ominous thunder clouds and we were in for one motherless gale as we entered the Gulf of Carpentaria.

For the next three days we got pounded by colossal ten metre swell which threw the boat about like a rag doll. During the most brutal twenty-four hours of the storm, the wind speed averaged fifty knots and we sailed with bare poles. The yacht's hull provided enough surface area for the wind to drive us along at ten knots, even though we had nothing but a handkerchief up on the bow for steerage. At the height of the storm's fury our wind instruments maxed out on a gust of sixty knots, only four knots below hurricane force, but Giampi took it all on the chin like a champ and never flinched. At no point during the tempest did I feel unsafe or that the boat was out of control.

It just goes to show, even though it was the most powerful storm I'd ever faced, when you're on a well-designed boat with a competent skipper and an experienced crew, you can sleep easy - that is to say when you're not being bounced off the ceiling of your cabin by the rolling waves - knowing that in all likelihood, everything will be ok.

We rode out the storm in relative safety and continued on our merry way.

We were all rather tired after the storm and spent the next few days catching up on sleep when we weren't on watch. One afternoon, while I was taking a nap in my cabin, I was woken up by Ralf howling with joy on deck.

'Get up here now boys,' he shouted in his thick, German accent.

Massimo and I raced into the cockpit to witness an unforgettable sight. We could see white splashes all the way to the horizon making their way towards us. More than five hundred creatures were making a beeline for the boat in what's known as a super pod, when smaller groups of dolphins' band together to form a huge mob and within minutes we were surrounded. The forerunners swept beside the boat, catching the bow wave before continuing on their way out to deeper water to hunt, stunning in their speed, grace and agility. For a quarter of an hour they sped past Giampi, whistling in delight as we whooped with joy to see such a phenomenal spectacle. It was a wonderful welcome to Australia, buoying our sprits after the battering from the storm and we arrived in Darwin safe and sound a couple of days later.

With two months to kill before the arrival of Aliena in Darwin I had plenty of time to explore. Darwin, in the Northern Territories isn't on most people's travel itinerary when they head to Australia and it was certainly different from any other place I'd ever been to.

The area is pretty much the last outpost for the aboriginal people who once ranged across the whole continent. A spiritual people, the aboriginals believe in Dreamtime, the foundation of their religion and culture for the last 65,000 years. Dreamtime is their story of the universe and how man came to be. It tells of how the creator intended for man to live in harmony with the world he found himself in, but this dream has changed into a nightmare and it was heart-breaking to witness the devastating effects alcoholism has on their communities. Our marina, situated on the outskirts of the city, was about a forty-minute walk from the town centre and wound its way through the rougher end of town. From early morning to late at night, all of the aboriginal people I saw were drinking, and I mean Drinking with a capital D. Beer for breakfast, lunch and dinner seemed to be the order of the day, every day, seven days a week. By noon there were dozens of drunks shouting and screaming at each other in front of their decrepit social housing projects and a few hours later they'd take to the streets and start battering each other. Men and women alike would be smacking each other around in drunken rage; a terribly sad thing to see.

One evening a glass bottle came whizzing through the air, smashing against the wall a couple of metres in front of me, followed by some garbled insult from an elderly man who promptly passed out across the street.

The aboriginals, once proud and self-sufficient people who thrived in the harsh outback, have been reduced to abject poverty and living in filth. It made me sick to my stomach to see such misery, yet another culture based on living in harmony with nature exploited until race crumbles into ashes.

I had little incentive to hang around, especially as I couldn't even swim in the ocean for fear of being bitten by a saltwater crocodile, munched by a great white shark or stung by box jellyfish. It seemed everything in Darwin wanted to kill me.

I'd managed to get hold of Stephen and Belle (the couple Sheila and I had partied with during the Panama Carnival) and they'd invited me to stay with them in Perth for as long as I wanted. After stashing

my sailing gear in storage and saying my goodbyes to
Massimo and Ralf, I hopped on a plane and flew to the
west coast. Stephen picked me up at the airport and
got straight down to business.

'So, what's your plan mate?' He enquired with
typical Australian frankness.

'I don't really have one. Just thought I'd hang out
with you guys for a while.'

'We've both taken the week off work. We thought
we'd take you down to Margaret River where both
our families have holiday homes. It's God's country
down there as long as you like surfing and drinking
wine. What d'ya reckon?'

'That sounds awesome mate. I'm always game.'

'Sweet,' he replied and after a short pause asked,
'can you drive?'

'Well, I had about half a dozen beers on the plane so
probably not.'

'Not now you idiot!' He laughed as he climbed up
into the driver's seat of a massive Toyota Land
Cruiser, completely kitted out for hard core off-
roading, 'you've got a driving licence, right?'

'Yeah, of course. I'm South African mate, we don't
have any public transport. I've been driving for almost
twenty years.'

'Well, I've got an idea. Belle and I have to go back to
work next week so instead of you hanging around in
Perth, do you fancy a road trip down the coast in this
beast,' he said as he lovingly patted the dashboard, 'I
won't be needing her for a month and she'll take you
just about anywhere.'

'Are you serious?'

'When have you ever seen me not be serious,' he
asked with a stupid grin on his face.

Flashbacks of the two of us running around - from Colombia to Tahiti - wearing capes and pretending to be superheroes sprang to mind as we both burst out laughing.

'I've driven her over fifteen thousand kilometres all the way around the country and she is due another adventure. If you want her for your stay, she's yours.'

It wasn't a difficult decision to make. Armed with a four-wheel drive weapon fit for a king meant another epic road trip beckoned and I signed up immediately.

After a few days exploring Perth, the three of us drove down to Margaret River in separate cars and we had a wonderfully debauched time eating fine foods, drinking finer wines and surfing the finest waves.

Well, that wasn't strictly true.

Belle had fallen pregnant at some point during the sailing trip, so she copped the designated driver spot and had to watch us drink her share. This left Stephen and me free to be as ridiculous as we wanted, just like old times, and most nights we ended up laughing in a hedge somewhere as we took it in turns to rugby tackle each other into any offensive foliage. At the end of the weekend Stephen and Belle had to return to work and headed back to Perth, but the following day reinforcements arrived by way of Stephen's brother, Kim Feast and his buddy Lewy Finnegan.

I was soon to find out they were the real deal in international bodyboarding. Kim had been ranked world number one for Drop Knee and Lewy was a serious charger on the world tour, so much so that Kelly Slater, the most dominant competitive surfer of all time, posted one of Lewy's videos on his Facebook page and stated, 'Boogers charge. And find better waves. Shit.'

Which roughly translates to 'elite bodyboarders are pushing the boundaries of what was thought possible on monster waves!'

A pro surfer posting a bodyboarding video is almost unheard of and Kelly Slater doing it is rarer still.

'Well mate, it's firing. You sure you're up for this?' Kim asked me as we gazed out to sea.

'It doesn't look that big,' I said with a little false bravado.

'That's because it's a two hundred metre paddle to get there. Trust me, we're not playing games today.'

We were talking about an infamous mutant of a wave, called the 'Box', breaking just off the coast. This monster wave, located in Margaret River, is a right-hand breaking slab of water that jacks up off a perilous limestone reef creating heavy, square shaped pits and extremely steep faces. Its thick lip is capable of hurling a surfer straight onto a rocky shelf covered in only a few inches of water. With a seriously quick take-off, you have to be fully committed if you're going to make it and if you get it wrong, you're history. Regarded by many as stupidly dangerous, I'm glad I didn't really know what I was getting myself into at the time.

'I didn't get dressed up for nothing,' I replied as we followed Lewy's footprints in the sand.

We walked down the beach as Kim gave me some final instructions while I put on my fins and strapped on my arm leash.

'Just follow me out over the reef. It gets quite shallow and it's a super low tide, so we'll have to scramble our way over some rocks too,' he said, 'paddle around the back of the wave and don't get caught too deep or you'll get destroyed.'

'Thanks mate.'

'I'll show you exactly where the line-up is. You need to take off from way wider than you'd think and sling shot yourself into the wave otherwise it's so steep it'll just fling you onto the reef.'

Great, I thought to myself. This sounds like it may permanently shorten my lifespan.

With mounting trepidation, I entered the water and started to paddle. We made our way through channels in the reef, all the while the roar of a mighty wave breaking grew louder and louder. My heart began to pound as we entered open water and I saw the Box up close and personal for the first time. Breaking around a crescent shaped reef, it just seemed to jack up out of nowhere. I watched a surfer paddle powerfully for the next wave. He popped up effortlessly, whipped down the face of an almost vertical wall of water, then disappear under the lip of the hollowest and gnarliest looking wave I'd ever seen.

A few seconds later he reappeared from deep inside the barrel churning well above his head, screamed in delight as he popped over the shoulder of the wave and landed safely in the channel next to a jet ski and two film crews in the water.

'He made that look easy,' I shouted to Kim in awe over the thundering water.

'Yeah, he certainly does. That's my mate Creed McTaggart. He's a free rider sponsored by Billabong to make surf movies all around the world. He's rad. Follow me, I'll introduce you.'

We paddled our way around the back of the wave and caught up with Lewy, Creed and only one other surfer, all sitting on their boards, waiting for the next big set to roll in. Kim introduced me and we all chatted for a couple of minutes.

'Lewy was just saying this is your first-time bodyboarding the Box. Is that correct?' Creed asked.

I nodded.

'It's a daunting wave bro, so maybe it's best to just watch us catch a few first. It's really important you take off from the correct spot or things could go catastrophic real quick,' he shouted over his shoulder as he paddled for his next wave.

He timed it perfectly, dropped down the face and out of sight and popped out the other side of another perfect overhead barrel in a cloud of spray a few seconds later.

I took his advice and watched the others surf for the next twenty minutes until I thought I was confident enough to have a go myself. The next group of big waves rolled in and I started paddling on the last of the three waves. If you mess up on the first wave you get pounded by the next two in quick succession, so taking off on the last wave mitigates a bit of the risk. I turned my board towards shore and began kicking my legs for all I was worth. After a few seconds I felt the unmistakable sensation of being driven forward as the wave surged, and to my horror I gazed down onto what looked like certain death. Ahead of me, under the glimmering water, I could see the outline of submerged rocks as the water boiled with rings of bubbles rising to the surface. It was one of the scariest things I've ever witnessed in the ocean and I immediately pulled back from the lip and paddled back to the boys sitting safely out at sea.

'You must be fucking joking,' I exclaimed in shock, 'that's a death trap!'

'We warned you this is a serious wave bro,' Lewy chipped in as the rest of the guys had a laugh at my expense.

Over the next half hour, I paddled into another handful of waves and pulled up short every time when I gazed down in fear onto the sinister reef. I am not ashamed to admit it was the most scared I'd ever been in my life other than the first time I went sky diving.

After an hour in the water I hadn't caught a wave and Kim paddled over.

'Dude, there's no shame in calling it a day. You've paddled out and seen the fury of this beast. None of us will think any less of you if you don't catch a wave here today.'

'I'm pretty scared man,' I admitted, 'I've never seen anything like this before, but I know if I don't at least give it a go then I'll regret it for the rest of my life.'

There and then I vowed to myself that the next wave that rolled in was mine, make or break. I didn't have long to wait as we all spotted another big set of waves rolling in from the ocean. Before I could change my mind, I turned, paddled hard and dropped in over the edge of the wave to wild cheers reverberating from behind me. Now fully committed there was no turning back as I dug the right-hand side rail of my bodyboard into the near vertical face of the wave and charged down it at a heart stopping speed. I bounced clear of the water, feeling my legs flailing behind me, but I just managed to land without digging the board's nose into the water and regained a semblance of control, tucking under the monumental lip of the wave as it came crashing down from above. For a couple of seconds I found myself in a perfect blue barrel of water, rushing headlong toward a diminishing circle of light ahead. The noise was thunderous as I gazed up in awe, entombed in the cavernous belly of the beast as the wave closed out in front of me. My world was instantaneously plunged into darkness and a millisecond later my board was ripped from my grasp. The wave's power was immense and it flung me around like a piece of lint in a giant washing machine, tightly curled in a ball with the piercing pain of unequalised ears as I was driven towards the ocean floor. I have no idea for how long I was underwater, but by the time I made it to the surface and the loving embrace of sunlight it felt like it had been an eternity and I gasped for breath. I scrambled for my board and paddled like hell as wall after wall of white-water rolled over me before I made it, unscathed, back to the safety of the channel.

My first wave on the Box

With an ear to ear smile and adrenaline still coursing through my veins I made my victorious paddle back to the line-up, passing Tom Jennings, one of the cameramen in the water who shouted in excitement, 'well done dude, you caught your first wave at the Box and you didn't fucking die!'

I got a heart-warming cheer from the boys and they all congratulated me when I arrived back.

'Jesus, that was scary,' I exclaimed, 'how big do you reckon that wave was?'

'That was a beauty mate. Four, maybe five foot,' Lewy replied.

'No way,' I said, 'I could have easily stood up inside that tube and I'm five foot eight.'

They went on to explain that in Western Australia they measure in the Hawaiian scale which is from behind the wave. To get the face height you simply double it. So I'd just ridden an eight to ten-foot monster. I caught one more wave that session to prove to myself that the first one hadn't been a fluke before calling it a day. Enough was enough. I'd survived the Box twice and I had nothing left to prove.

You would struggle to find three nicer guys at a surf break anywhere in the world and I thanked Kim, Lewy and Creed for their help and advice on the paddle home.

Back on the safety of dry land Kim turned to me and said, 'Well mate, I can confirm that you're a madman. By our normal standards, that was really dangerous out there today. I'm proud you had the balls to take a crack at it.'

And so was I. I'd confronted my fear head on, taken the plunge and survived the scariest wave of my life. Another epic experience forever deposited in the 'Bank of Rad.'

Chapter 16

Snowy Mountains

36°27'15S, 148°15'45E

Over the next couple of days Kim, Lewy and I cruised up and down the coast in search of the perfect wave. Equipped with Stephen's mammoth Land Cruiser we accessed some of Australia's most isolated beaches and without another soul in sight, we surfed to our hearts' content. Uncrowded surf breaks are uncommon in this day and age, but completely empty ones are the thing of dreams. It was just me, my board and a couple of friends enjoying the ocean's free gift of perfectly peeling waves. No crowds, no pollution and not a care in the world. After a few days the big swell died down and the boys headed back to Perth, but for the next fortnight I explored innumerable pristine white sandy beaches and crystal-clear waters and enjoyed the peace and quiet of keeping my own company again. As much as I love sailing, the constant contact with the same people is wearing after a while, so it was the perfect opportunity to reconnect with myself and recharge my batteries. After a day spent exploring, each night I'd sample a different bottle of exquisite wine from the world-renowned vineyards of the Margaret River region while I read a book. I'd gaze out to sea and spot humpbacks and southern right whales frolicking in the shallows, until the light faded and I retired to sleep in comfort in the back of the truck. It was a blissful time to reflect on how far I'd come as I discovered another continent on the opposite side of the world from where I'd set off.

Another deserted beach in South Western Australia

With a month left before the arrival of Aliena in Darwin, I headed to Brisbane to chill out with one of my best mates, Matthew Dibble. A former professional rugby player, Matt has thighs the thickness of my waist and a heart to match. He's one of the funniest and most genuinely kind human beings I know, and just like me, he loves to drink and party. Being ginger, Welsh and on the heavier side of the scales, he really isn't built for the heat. So armed with a crate of Victoria Bitter, we vegetated on the couch in air-conditioned luxury each day and watched back to back seasons of The Walking Dead. Sometimes it's just awesome to have nothing to do and I hadn't realised how much I'd missed the banter and familiarity of just hanging out with an old friend.

My liver and kidneys couldn't take much more abuse though, so after a week it was time to get moving again and I flew to Sydney. Craig Arnold, another of my best friends, is an absolute legend just like Dibble, but for different reasons.

'You're my boy, Blue!'

I heard Craig's unmistakable holler closely followed by a bone crunching man hug as he literally picked me up from the airport. 'Welcome back to Sydney, brother.'

After my shipwreck debacle in Portugal I'd flown out to Australia and stayed with Craig and his brother David for a month before heading to New Zealand. Craig's the most optimistic, vibrant and driven man I've ever met and the cofounder of an incredible community driven gym franchise called Core9. Just the kind of guy you need to hang out with when you need a pure shot of positivity.

'I've managed to take five days off work for the first time this year so how do you fancy doing a little reconnaissance trip with me in the mountains?' Craig asked.

'Yeah, that sounds brilliant,' I replied with a tinge of fear, 'can you first define 'little' though.'

At ninety kilograms of pure chiselled muscle, backed up with one hundred percent commitment to anything he does, when Craig puts his mind to something it gets done. The thought of giving up has never crossed his mind and this attitude made him the perfect candidate to captain the Australian Adventure Racing Team. Adventure Racing is the pinnacle of elite endurance sport where a team of like-minded fucking maniacs take on Herculean challenges.

The last race he'd entered with his team was traversing Tasmania in a week - running, cycling, climbing and kayaking their way across some of the most inaccessible and inhospitable terrain in the world. Snatching a few minutes of sleep along the way, they pushed their bodies to breaking point and just kept on going, kilometre after relentless kilometre, day and night until they hit the finish line.

At one stage during the race Craig lost his eyesight after drinking too much water. The man went blind! Although he didn't know it at the time, he'd flushed out all of his body's electrolytes. Any sane person would have thrown in the towel and headed for the hospital but not Craig, I don't think there is anything on earth that could stop him. Refusing to let his team mates down, he gripped the backpack of the person in front of him while the guy behind him told him where to put his feet and they marched on. I cannot imagine the sheer mental strength required to endure such a terrifying situation, but he soldiered on for three hours and eighteen kilometres more until he collapsed with hypernatremia and hyperthermia in a mountain hut. Despite the request from a Search and Rescue team for him to quit, he refused their assistance as that meant instant disqualification. Two hours later, after a little nap, his sight returned and he charged on. They finished the race pushing a delirious team member - who had also succumbed to hypernatremia - in a shopping trolley, before bundling him into a kayak for the last leg of the six-hundred-kilometre race where he was whisked off to the hospital. To put it mildly, Craig puts the hard into hardcore, so my trepidation was well-founded.

'Fifty, maybe sixty kilometres over four days mate… easy peasy,' he smiled at me with a mischievous glint in his eye.

Fifty or sixty kilometres in four days didn't sound too bad but Craig was up to something and I could sense an imminent beasting.

We were about to head into the Snowy Mountains and in midwinter conditions it wasn't a joke. That evening was spent checking all of our equipment and Craig made me practice putting up his four-season tent on my own. He said if anything untoward happened to him on the trek it would be my responsibility to take charge.

'What do you mean untoward? I asked.

He grinned at me, 'if I should die.'

I laughed, 'stop pissing about man.'

'Seriously,' he said, 'make sure the tent is always clipped to your body before you're convinced it's safely secured to the snow. One gust of wind could rip it from your hands and that's a death sentence,' he repeated more than once, 'and nothing sharp goes anywhere near the tent fabric. A slip with your ice axe or a careless kick with your crampons and we're in a world of trouble.'

Having recently trekked for thirty-six days across a Patagonian ice shelf the dude knew his stuff and I listened to all his advice intently. Even though I'd been on dozens of camping expeditions, surviving in the snow required a completely different set of skills and I had a whole lot to learn.

With a large backpack each plus food and cooking gear in a separate bag we'd drag along behind us on a sled, we were all set.

We left early the next morning for Threadbo, the closest ski resort to our destination. I rented some mountain boots, snowshoes and a set of crampons before we jumped on a chair lift which took us up to the trek's access point.

What greeted us at the top of the lift literally took my breath away. Down in the valley we were sheltered from the wind, but on the plateau there was nothing to stop the ninety kilometre an hour head winds from almost blowing me off my feet.

'Jesus Christ,' I screamed at Craig as the wind whipped my words away, 'this is insane!'

With a manic laugh followed by a muffled shout of 'this is what we were born for brother,' Craig set off trailblazing through thigh deep snow, pulling both the sled and me behind him like some sort of bionic super mule.

We were both bent over double to give the wind as little surface area as possible to batter our bodies, slogging our way through nightmarish conditions to the deafening accompaniment of a screaming gale. With head down to preserve my face from the stinging bite of the horizontally driven snow I once again asked myself, what the hell have you got yourself into this time?

I'd prefer not to remember how many times I fell or was blown over, but each time Craig patiently stopped and waited for me to dust myself off before setting off again. Each step was exhausting as the deep snow weighed heavily on top of my snowshoes. I was forced to lift my knees high and get my foot above the snow before plunging it down again, otherwise I'd catch my toe and fall over again, expending yet more energy trying to get back to my feet.

During our first short break, huddled together behind a rock for a little protection from the wind, we munched on energy bars to keep our strength up. We were burning hundreds of calories an hour just trying to stay warm in temperatures of minus fifteen degrees with the wind chill factor, never mind the energy required to keep moving forward.

Craig's pace was relentless. Time and again I lagged behind him even though I was pushing my body to the max.

'Sorry bro,' I said, 'I feel like I'm holding you up,' I confessed as my teeth clattered together from the cold. With five layers of clothing on, my temperature was just about right when we were moving but within a minute of stopping I was frozen to the core.

'Don't be ridiculous Dazzla, these are brutal conditions and you're smashing it. Just remember, baby steps. One foot in front of the other. Don't focus on anything else.'

We marched for eight hours that day, the longest sixteen kilometres of my life. By the end of it I could barely lift my snowshoes off the ground as my hip flexors screamed in agony with every step.

Never had I ever been so happy to hear the words, 'This is it mate, welcome to our campsite for the night.'

We were on a plateau and completely surrounded by mountains. Other than the outline of distant trees and some dark rocks breaking the surface, everything else around us was covered in pure white snow. For the first time in the whole day I could see more than fifty metres in front of me as the skies cleared and the wind stopped howling. I flopped down onto my backpack, close to exhaustion and my body screamed 'no more', but if I thought the day's trials were over I had another thing coming.

Home sweet home in the Snowy Mountains

'Right Daz, we need to build a snow wall now,' Craig announced.

'A fucking snow wall?' I groaned.

'Yeah man, to protect the tent from the wind. It may have let up for the moment, but it'll be howling again tonight.'

Craig explained that we needed to chop out blocks of snow to create a wall ten-foot-wide by five-foot-high - an impenetrable barrier that would ensure that we survived the night. I didn't need more encouragement than that and after another energy bar we set to work. It took us the best part of an hour and a half for the snow wall, which was unbelievably strong by the time we finished.

Then it was time to put the tent up. In snow, pegs are useless so instead you use little squares of fabric with loops of chord on them. Once buried, you pull on the loops and they dig into the snow like inverted little parachutes, anchoring the tent securely. The digging wasn't finished though, as we still had to burrow out a separate cooking area and a depression at the entrance to the tent to enable the easy removal of our boots. By the time we finished I was wilting like a precious little flower and we hadn't even prepared dinner yet. The food took another hour as we melted snow to cook with as well as rehydrate ourselves as my mouth was as dry as Gandhi's flip flops. I was freezing cold and to add insult to injury, I desperately needed to take a dump.

I won't go into the logistics of a snow poo, but suffice to say it required a little more digging, just in case I hadn't already made enough holes in the snow for one day.

Even taking a shit in snow takes up a ridiculous amount of time. It amazed me how everything took four times longer to achieve with the debilitating effect the cold had on my dexterity and overall coordination. To do anything I'd take my gloves off for thirty seconds, fumble them back on again and then bury my hands in my armpits, until a few minutes later a stabbing pain reminded me they were still attached to my arms. I may be painting a rather bleak picture but as I sat on a Therma-rest, wearing every item of clothing I possessed and huddled under a sleeping bag next to Craig, colder than I'd ever been in my life, I wouldn't have traded places with anybody else in the world.

To see Craig wholly attuned to his environment, with all his winter survival systems honed from months of practice, was a beautiful thing to see and the portion of steaming pasta and sauce I ate that evening was one of the most deliciously satisfying meals of my entire life.

After dinner we scraped the cooking utensils clean with handfuls of fresh snow and retired to the tent, still fully clothed except for our boots and burrowed into our sleeping bags. It began to snow again and the wind picked up strength.

'You're gonna love this bit mate,' Craig chimed in ten minutes later, 'now that you've warmed up a bit, grab the inners from inside your boots, your gloves and woollen hat and stuff them all in your sleeping bag.'

'You're kidding me, they're soaking wet and freezing cold.'

Craig laughed loudly and said, 'Afraid not mate, trust me. Otherwise they'll freeze overnight and you'll be screwed tomorrow.'

'Another death sentence perhaps?'

'Nah, just a little frostbite if you're unlucky.'

I pulled the wet gear into my sleeping bag. It had exactly the opposite effect of a hot water bottle and my balls retracted a couple more inches.

'How the hell did you do this for over a month bro?' I asked flabbergasted.

'It's amazing what you can get used to, given enough time and a sunny disposition,' he replied with big grin. And yet, in no time at all, our body heat warmed the tent and I gradually stripped layer after layer of clothing off until I was down to my thermals.

'I never thought I'd ever feel warm again,' I sighed with contentment.

'Don't get too comfortable buddy,' he answered with a chuckle, 'every couple of hours we have to take it in turns to head outside.'

'What?'

'Yeah, we need to clear the snow from the top of the tent, otherwise it will collapse under the weight and we'll be buried alive.'

Great, I thought to myself, this is some sort of sadomasochism in the snow.

I slept remarkably well, all things considered, and woke up feeling fresh the next morning to clear blue skies. I cleared the tent somewhere around midnight and Craig followed up a few hours later. There was a foot of fresh snow around the tent and a couple of inches on the roof but at least the wind had died down. We prepared breakfast and melted a lot more snow before breaking camp and setting off an hour later towards a place called Seaman's Hut, one of the mountain shelters.

By lunchtime the blue skies had disappeared and we were once again lashed by horizontally driven snow as we trudged our way uphill. Late afternoon, through a brief break in the cloud, we both spotted a forlorn looking figure making his way up the mountain ahead of us.

Craig pointed at him, 'Man, he must be an elite athlete. He's travelling super light and probably trying to get to the summit and back before sundown. He doesn't even have a backpack on and it's close to dark so he's cutting it fine.'

Over the next few hours this apparition appeared and then disappeared again behind a veil of clouds, always the same distance ahead of us and we sensed something wasn't quite right.

'He should be moving way quicker than that, shouldn't he?' I asked Craig.

'Yeah, for sure,' he replied in a troubled tone.

The hut finally appeared and we made our way inside to find another team of mountaineers plus the apparition, an elderly man in his seventies. He was blue from the cold and shivering in the corner under a mountain of clothes.

After quick introductions the other two chaps asked us if the old boy was with us.

'No,' we replied, shaking our heads.

'We've just been tracking him up the mountain for the last couple of hours,' I said.

'Well, he stumbled into the hut about a quarter of an hour go,' one of the mountaineers said, 'he's delirious and was only wearing a tee shirt and raincoat.'

'No way,' Craig said.

'Yep, he's wearing boots, crampons and a pair of trousers that look older than him. He's got no food, water or compass. Not even a head torch. We've been trying to feed him and warm him up but he's unresponsive. I'm a medical doctor and this is pretty serious.'

Over the next hour, as we thawed him out and fed him our spare food, his story slowly surfaced. Thirty years ago, in his prime, he'd hiked up to the hut and back down again in one day. He thought he was still capable of repeating the feat and set out early that morning in clear conditions, with only a couple of chocolate bars and a bottle of water for the day. By some miracle he found the hut, but if neither of our parties had holed up there for the evening, there is no doubt he'd have frozen to death overnight. The poor chap had no idea of the level of danger he'd put himself in. After hearing his story and ascertaining the old fellow was mentally unsound, the doctor made an executive decision and called in mountain rescue for an immediate evacuation. Within the hour he was whisked off the mountain and reunited with his frantically worried daughter down in the valley. A couple of hours later we got the call to say he was safe and it came as a huge relief to us all.

Sleeping in the hut was actually colder than being in the tent, but it was a welcome relief to do without the two hours of digging and late-night snow clearing, and after a while I warmed up and slept like a baby. The next morning, I woke up to an incredible pink sunrise with only a few wispy clouds in an otherwise beautiful blue sky. After leaving the hut, I gazed around in awe at three hundred and sixty degrees of pristine, snowy white mountains. It felt rather eerie at first until I registered the change. Other than the crunching of snow underfoot, there was complete and utter silence. The gale had blown itself out and there wasn't a breath of air to disturb the ethereal tranquillity. We'd planned to head up to the top of Mount Kosciuszko and it was the perfect weather for a summit day.

Mount 'Kozzy` was named by a Polish Count who first explored the Australian Alps back in 1840, in honour of a famous Polish-Lithuanian freedom fighter, General Tadeusz Kościuszko.

At 2228 metres above sea level it's a quarter the height of Mount Everest, but the two mountains share a common distinction. Even though it was hardly a steep hill and we strolled up to the top barely breaking a sweat, the summit of Mount Kosciuszko is the highest point on the Australian continent, just like Everest is the highest in Asia (and the world for that matter). While we stood atop a continent, arm in arm, we both howled to the heavens in joy. It may not have been the highest peak either of us had been up, but we'd done it together and it was a special moment.

Craig wanted to do some ice-climbing the next day so after sliding back down Mount Kosciuszko on the sled, we walked a further ten kilometres to another flat plateau near some ice cliffs, but I had a major problem. Within an hour of setting off from Kozzy my feet started to hurt, and by the time we made camp I was in excruciating pain. Rented boots are never comfortable so I hobbled my way through the day, putting on a brave face, but underneath that thin veneer I was in agony. By the time we stopped I could barely stand, and I was getting worried. I could not imagine anything more embarrassing than having to get a mountain rescue for sore feet, but there was no way I could have taken another two days of hiking in that much pain.

'You've been very quiet today buddy,' Craig noted as we crawled our way into the tent, 'are your feet still giving you grief?'

'Yip, I've never felt this much pain in my feet before.'

I confided in him as we sat in the front entrance and took off our boots. Thoughts of frostbite and missing toes weren't far from my mind.

'Oh my God, you won't believe this mate,' I cried out in consternation, 'I'm a compete idiot.'

As I pulled my throbbing feet out of the hard, outer encasement of the mountain boots I looked down in disbelief. On my right foot I was wearing the left inner boot and vise versa on the other foot. For a whole day's hiking, both my feet were twisted in the wrong direction.

Craig just burst out laughing.

'Well, look on the bright side, that's a mistake you'll never make again.'

I fell asleep that night to the strangely soothing sound of Craig chuckling to himself, feeling one-part idiot but four-parts relieved I wasn't going to cripple myself or lose any toes. We woke up the next morning to a complete whiteout. You couldn't see more than ten metres in any direction as everything was blanketed in a thick, grey fog. With zero visibility and the temperature still Baltic we were confined to our tent all day, and I have to admit I was secretly rather chuffed because my feet felt like they'd been run over by a steam roller. If you ever find yourself squeezed shoulder to shoulder next to a buddy in a claustrophobic little tent for twenty four hours, and neither of you ever run out of anything interesting to talk about (except when you're snoozing or sleeping of course), then you know you have found a true friendship that will last the test of time.

With hours to kill we spoke about anything and everything. From our ambitions and goals, to future adventure plans, relationships, love, loss and questions of what the point of life was anyway. We finally concluded we didn't know all the answers, but we knew what we both held dearest was our personal freedom to go and do whatever made us happy, and that was enough for us. Somewhere in the midst of one of our philosophical debates Craig blurted out. 'Bro, why don't you write a book about your experiences?'

'Seriously Craig, who on earth would want to read about me. I'm not famous or extreme enough to warrant anybody's attention.'

'Bullshit man, the problem with people like you and me is all the things we push ourselves to do seem totally normal to us. But they aren't normal when you compare them to most other people's activities. I don't know anybody else who lived in a van for years to save up enough money to buy a boat, then got shipwrecked. He didn't give up and found a new avenue to follow his dream of sailing around the world by crewing on other people's boats. You've followed the sun for five years and now you're halfway around the world, up a mountain freezing your balls off in a tent, hiking midwinter in the Australian Alps with me on an endless quest for new adventures and experiences. It would make a great book.'

'I'm not so sure man.'

'It's inspirational stuff mate and I'd want to read about it. Everybody is capable of doing incredible things, but most people just don't know it yet. All they need is a little nudge in the right direction, to read a book about all the stuff you've been through and how it all came about.'

'I don't know, I'd have to think about it.'

As I mulled it over throughout the rest of the day, I acknowledged to myself that I'd always wanted to write a book, and Craig was right, now I had something to write about so it was time to take the plunge.

'I'm going to do it brother. I'm going to write an adventure book about my travels!' I stated with absolute conviction later that evening.

Craig looked up from stirring dinner and starred me straight in the eye.

'Yeah man, I know you will,' he replied matter-of-factly as he clasped my shoulder in one of his meaty paws. 'Tell me something I don't know. Everything you've ever said you'd do, you've accomplished, so this will be no different.'

So Craig, here it is, my brother from another mother, my book (although there's three of them) as promised. Come what may I'll always be a man of my word, so just as you confirmed in that frosty tent, if I say I'll do something it's as good as done, but regardless, thanks for the little nudge in the right direction.

The next day dawned with a spectacular blue sky. Without a cloud in sight we packed up all our ice encrusted belongings for the last time and took a leisurely stroll across the plateau until we hit the chair lift and headed back down to the valley floor. I took my boots off for the final time (with the inners on the correct feet I'd just like to add) and was close to orgasmic as I stripped off, stuffing the clothes I'd worn for days into a bin liner before they decided to walk off on their own accord. There are few simple pleasures in life better than exchanging four-day old crusty camping clothes for soft and sweet-smelling clean ones. We headed straight to a bar for a celebratory pie and beer and I delighted in the luxury of once again being warm. It had been another memorable adventure with one of the most spectacular people I know. I'm very privileged to be able to call Craig my brother, a friend who knows all about my past and believes in my future, accepting me warts and all. My only bug bear is that I don't get to hang out with the guy often enough.

As Hemingway once said, sweet is the memory of distant friends, like the mellow rays of the departing sun it falls tenderly, yet sadly on the heart.

Book 3

Chapter 1

The Magnet
08°44'30S,115°12'45E

With my walkabout around Australia complete, I flew back north from Sydney to Darwin, meeting up with my new skipper Miguel, his wife Carmen and the other member of the crew, Johan. I hadn't spent much time with Miguel and Carmen over the course of the WARC as they were, shall we say, slightly more conservative than me so our paths hadn't crossed on the party scene. Both in their mid-sixties, quite reserved and very Spanish, it didn't seem at first like it would be a good fit. I was used to sailing with people of around about my own age and of a similar outlook on life but they were very traditional and old enough to be my parents. I hadn't spent too much time with Johan either. He was a middle-aged Swedish computer programmer whose first real traveling experience was this trip around the world. I have to give him top points for jumping straight in at the adventure deep end, but in all honesty we had little in common. The three of them had sailed together for almost a year so I felt like an outsider when I first arrived. On the plus side though, Aliena was a stunning Oyster 56, a true top end blue-water cruiser and one of the most beautifully designed boats in the world. With long and chic teak decks the top sides were immaculate and below decks she was the size of a well-appointed apartment with three large cabins, a huge saloon, a dining table that seated eight and all the mod cons you'd expect to get on a boat that cost well in excess of a million pounds. Aliena is the type of boat your average sailor can only ever dream of owning and I fell in love with her immediately.

The first leg of our journey was the thousand mile sail to Bali and we had plenty of time to get to know each other as we set off together to cross the Timor Sea in high spirits. Even though I'd felt a bit like a fish out of water during the preparations for the voyage in Darwin, within a couple of days of being back at sea I felt right at home again. Miguel loved sailing, but he loved his boat even more and we hit it off immediately. He derived enormous pleasure from showing me every nook and cranny of his beloved Aliena - named after his two granddaughters Alicia and Elena - and we quickly developed a close friendship based on mutual trust and respect. Although Carmen and I struggled to communicate at first due to her poor English and my non-existent

Spanish, she went out of her way to make me feel welcome. You'd struggle to find a kinder and more generous couple than Miguel and Carmen and it turned out I hit the jackpot with them as my new 'owners'.

It was plain sailing for the whole trip except for one memorable episode. Around 8am one morning near the end of the voyage, I was off watch and comfortably ensconced in my palatial cabin reading a book, when I was violently thrown off my top bunk and slammed into the cabin door. As I picked myself up, I was flung in the opposite direction and bounced off my bed. With images of a ruptured hull from a collision with a submerged container whizzing through my mind, I pinged my way through the saloon like some sort of human ball in a giant pinball machine, rebounding off every available surface as my world pitched in every direction, the boat bucking like a bull gone mad and shaking like somebody having a seizure.

Printed in Great Britain
by Amazon